DARE TO WIN
MAGIC MATRAS
to
MOTIVATE YOURSELF

DARE TO WIN

MAGIC MATRAS *to* MOTIVATE YOURSELF

ANANDI LAL MALANI

PENTAGON PRESS
NEW DELHI

DARE TO WIN
MAGIC MATRAS TO MOTIVATE YOURSELF

First Published 2005

ISBN 81-86830-71-5

Published by
PENTAGON PRESS
101, AVG Bhawan, M-3, Connaught Circus,
New Delhi-110001 (India)
Phones: 011-23415198, 23415205 • Fax: 011-51517091
e-mail: rajanarya@vsnl.com

Printed by
ELEGANT PRINTERS
New Delhi-110064

Contents

Preface

"One cannot manage change. One can only be ahead of it." Says Peter Drucker. A world without barriers is changing faster and to achieve competitiveness to survive and excel in 21st century, each individual and organisation need to lead change, by performance excellence for value creation in all spheres. Professional Managers/Entrepreneurs for Corporate Success need to be best leaders, active team members, motivators, action oriented, optimum utilisers of all available resources, constantly impatient with the *status quo* and above all trend setters; to improve over all performance and results par excellence continuously one-after-another to achieve unmatchable productivity and quality at rock-bottom cost. Life is battlefield. Since the dawn of human history, consciously or unconsciously all are struggling to attain excellence, perfection and happiness. Life long journey, right from birth to death is considered as an uninterrupted persue to attain fulfillment of all desires. People break their own records and they surpass their own limits. You are passionate to offer result par excellence that deliver competitive advantage, as well as translate your thinking into solution and reality. Now, its your turn to lead revolution since a wise man can create more opportunities than he actually finds.

Most of us need some help to activate their life and become self-motivated comprising positive attitude, self-esteem, self-confidence with feeling of self-worth. A positive attitude means not bowing to the fear of failure but continue to make fresh efforts for success. You will realise that there has never been a problem except in your thinking. Each and everything starts with you. Without desires and dreams there can be no motivation. Communication is key to success and our communication skill adds value, meaning and effectiveness in all our roles. The effective communication helps to obtain motivation and willing involvement of team members. Things will move only when you announce time limits. Besides, it is intended to help you master the techniques specially in areas like efficient and effective day-to-day administration, setting goals to achieve the total organisational objectives, foster creativity and innovation at all levels, creative process of problem solving, continuous cost reduction, human resource development, personnel handling and evaluation and management of criticism etc. It contains ideas that will challenge and provoke you to assess improvement continuously in areas such as:

(i) Are our employees performing to their utmost potential and operating at peak efficiency?
(ii) Where do we under perform? How to enhance further the productivity of our employees?
(iii) How to enhance a more positive attitude of employees to deliver their best at all times?
(iv) How to develop multi-skills in employees to ensure their personal as well as professional growth?
(v) Are we making optimum use of all available resources? If not, how to overcome the obstacles?
(vi) Are our decisions the best one?

Better to take positive immediate action to correct inadequacies and keep your skills finely tuned to reach your destination. Overcome your weaknesses then all that is left are your strengths. Self-confidence develops as one builds on strengths and overcomes weaknesses. Your strength are of no value to you until and unless you put them to use. Determine, how you can use your strength to your best advantage. You always play to win and never try to lose. Winners do it differently to find new ways to do things, experiment it and push their limits to achieve the desired goals. That's what this book is all about. This book is unique not only for a selected few but for everyone from all walk of life. This will activate your life and make possible to find yourself several times better off than you were before.

As a human, you are the best creation of this universe. You are more capable to achieve all success than what you think you are. You are made to win. Start now. Here is the way you can DARE TO WIN.

ANANDI LAL MALANI

1

Inspiration from Lord Ganeshji—The Symbol of Wisdom and Success

THE IMPORTANCE OF INSPIRATION

Strong enthusiasm and emotions are necessary for achievement of goals, which gives courage to undertake the toughest journeys and inspire individuals to achieve the unthinkable. Inspiration is essential to achieve success and success knows no boundaries.

Inspiration can be defined as the inner state of a person, where the intellect conceives and appreciates a higher thought than our present level of development. Simultaneously, the mind supports it. The source of inspiration is just internal. This means that it arises at the level of mind and intellect within you.

Inspiration enables you to fix a goal or purpose in life so that your time and actions will become systematic as well as organised and you will become cheerful, enthusiastic and energetic. Then you will be able to save your mental energy from being diverted to unproductive channels to grow both materially and spiritually. Besides, you will become a source of inspiration to others.

CONDITION YOUR MIND

Mind is housed in the cage of the human body. The mind gets conditioned by the environment in which a man is brought up over a period of time. The period in fact commences right from the moment a baby is conceived in the mother's womb. Human mind is never empty but crowded and noisy. The mind remains busy and a lot of activity goes on there even when we are asleep and not engaged consciously. Mind accumulates and saves many experiences, feelings, emotions and so on through the five senses of the human body.

It is the mind that creates both the constructive and destructive impulses which generate conflicts. We must learn to choose our thoughts and decide which thoughts should dominate our mind. The first step is to bring it under control to redouble the energy of your mind and increase its capacity to think and concentrate. The second step is to break the chain of useless, irrelevant, purposeless thoughts and substitute it differently with new, purposeful and spiritual thoughts to attain the ultimate goal. In other words, a wise man is master of his mind who conserves his energy and directs it towards more productive ends to fulfill his dreams. Let your mind work for you.

INSPIRATION FROM LORD GANESHJI

From ancient times, the prayer to Lord Ganeshji is offered first and foremost as he is the famous "बुद्धिदाता" as well as "सिद्धिदाता"—the giver of 'Wisdom' and 'Success'. 'Sumukh' is the first name of Lord Ganeshji and his face gives us inspiration as under:

Big Head

- Knowledge is power. Knowledge is virtue.
- बुद्धिर्यस्य बलं तस्य, निर्बुद्धेस्तु कुतो बलम् ।
- Think no evil.
- Be positive in your thoughts and attitude. If you aim

at excellence; you can achieve it.

- Be creative for innovation.
- Have a vision and foresight.
- Be suitable and fittest in knowledge, will and skill.
- Be enlightened, committed, motivated, happy and healthy.
- Think big, think fast and think ahead.
- Think profitably.
- Concentrate on important and high return tasks.
- Set objective in key result areas.
- Use collective wisdom to achieve common goals.
  - Keep high energy level.
  - Always focus on the end results.
  - Take right decision even if tough.
- Do not confine your thinking to a defined mould. You can do things differently to implement great ideas.
- Strive hard for continuous improvement; particularly in the areas of quality, productivity, efficiency, effectiveness, profitability and turnover etc. to set example for the future.
- Turn the vision into well-defined and attainable objectives.
- Cut costs and add value by own creativity and wisdom.
- Use your Supreme thinking power for release of your creative power to solve the complex problems.
- Never stop thinking to invent, innovate and improve.
- If you think you can—you will.
- Think of working together.
- Think for competition.
- Think to increase customers.
- Think of improvement in everything you do.
- Think of high standard in everything you do.
- Act to achieve the objectives by properly managing the following Ms:

  (a) Man (b) Money

(c) Machines (d) Materials
(e) Methods (f) Market
(g) Minutes (h) Measurement
(i) Motivation (j) Motto.

- Attain the objectives and enjoy success.
- We all have one thing in common i.e. 24 hours a day which when properly used, will make all the difference.

Narrow Eyes

- Deep concentration to finish the task in hand well in time.
- See no evil.
- Overlook defects of others.

Big Ears

- Listen more. Encourage others to talk about themselves.
- Listen patiently to new ideas and suggestions from others.
- Listen actively.
- Separate the essential from the non-essential tasks and discriminate between what to do and what not to do.
- Eliminate unproductive practices and procedures first.
- Eliminate unnecessary work from the system.
- Search for different ways of solving problems.
- Hear no evil.

Long Nose

- Learn more.
- Learn continuously.
- Gather all important events from surroundings.

Small Mouth

- Analyse and evaluate

- Speak less. Nature has gifted us with two ears and one mouth, so that we listen more than we speak.
- Talk to the point.
- Speak to inspire, motivate and energise people to create courage, optimism and enthusiasm in them.
- Always focus on the end results to execute and deliver the results better than promised and work effectively to achieve high targets.
- Improve productivity, quality, value, profit, customer satisfaction, employees benefits and performance.
- Recognise your potential and exploit it.
- Argument is an extremely poor system of thinking since it is to do with win, lose, defence, attack and ego which are emotional things.
- Speak success stories to convince people skillfully.
- Congratulate and praise people for their achievements and success.
- Talk no evil.
- Do not criticise, condemn or complain but try to create the best.
- Give honest and sincere appreciation.
- If you are wrong, admit it quickly and emphatically.
- Develop positive attitude by proper understanding, self-confidence, patience and belief.
- Improve personality traits for positive attitude, some of which are enthusiasm, cheerfulness, sincerity, decisiveness, consideration, warmth, courage, friendliness, relaxation, optimism and courtesy.

One Teeth

- Fix up clear goals on the important and high return tasks for improvement to make things easier, better, faster and cheaper. Keep preserving on each goal till you succeed.
- Perfection is a journey. It does not stop at any definite target. Once goals are fixed, the targets are achieved. Then targets are revised and the journey continues.

CONCLUSION

Consistent efforts in maintaining and improving the inspiration level are essential to grow to a higher level of development. This helps to achieve peace, prosperity and ultimate spiritual enlightenment and avoid a dull and meaningless existence. When inspired, you are ready to think for yourself; i.e. how to compete, to collaborate, to use new ideas, to ensure optimum use of all available resources and to deliver your best at all times to achieve the over-all goals.

2

Efficient and Effective Day-to-Day Administration—A Miracle Technique

MANAGEMENT is a process aiming at action while ADMINISTRATION is the moving force or the policy guidelines to accomplish the task of management.

The VALUES, BELIEFS and ATTITUDES play a vital role in MANAGEMENT **PHILOSOPHY.** The key **MANAGEMENT FUNCTIONS** are: (i) Planning; (ii) Organising; (iii) Staffing; (iv) Budgeting; (v) Directing; (vi) Coordinating; (vii) Controlling; and (viii) Reporting. In order to achieve the excellent results and for successful completion of any job in an industry, the following need to be managed properly:

1. Men
2. Money
3. Machines
4. Materials
5. Methods
6. Market
7. Minutes
8. Measurement
9. Motivation
10. Motto

Have you ever said to yourself **"I did not have enough**

time". You are not alone, since you have exactly the same number of hours per day, equal to ALL SUCCESSFUL PEOPLE. Then **"How is it that you are not one of the successful people?"**

Time management is in fact self-management. You should learn to manage yourself in relation to time. Start your day with a "THINGS TO DO TODAY" list and prioritise the vital few, out of the entire jobs to be done. Consider **"How you can achieve the best results in relation to use of your time?"** You should plan your time to concentrate and ensure your maximum efforts on the **IMPORTANT AND HIGH RETURN TASKS.** You need to concentrate on results and not on being busy. Use your time efficiently and wisely.

The format will help you in your **"things to do today"** list. You must remember the following **tips to implement the same** on a **day-to-day basis.**

1. Get organised. One cannot do well, unless one gets organised. Be systematic in handling information.
2. It is what you learn, after you know that it all counts. Learning is a continuous process. For example, Charles Schwab of USA used to make a million dollars per year at par with Walter Chrysler. Once Charles Schwab asked a consultant to suggest how to get more done per day. The consultant spend a week with him and advised the following:
   "Every morning, write down what are the six most important things, you want to do on that day. Start doing the first one first and then the second and third. If by then the day is gone, next day add three more. Do it for one month and if it works, send me your payment." Charles Schwab sent him $ 25,000 after a month.
3. Do your thinking on paper. Maintain good documentation. You will make quicker and better decisions, if you write down the pros and cons of a line of action. Anything in black and white removes

ambiguity and operations run smoothly. This doesn't take time but it saves time. Recognize that every hour invested in effective planning, saves four in execution to obtain better results. Set measurable and time-bound objectives in Key Result Areas.

4. Set positive objectives with priorities. Break the jobs into small tasks. Do important jobs now before they become urgent. Set completion time for all important tasks.

5. Do it now, don't fear failure, be decisive. Read it once and dispose it of on first handling. Don't hoard it. I quote here a story "If I don't do, I don't get money." There lived an old man working hard at Railway Station who carried luggage of passengers across platform @ Rs. 10 per trip consisting upto 40 kg. When asked, "How many times per day you carry the luggage?" He said "As many times, as I can because the more times I carry, the more I get. If I don't do, I don't get money." That is why there is a management principle of "Piece Rate" and "No Work No Wages."

6. Plan and schedule your work. Plan for the unexpected and leave room for flexibility. Allow time between appointments. Take time to sharpen your axe to get more output than planned. Ensure to plan ahead your day realistically to complete the job systematically and in time.

7. Delegate, but don't forget. Budget your time. Time is money. Things will move only, when you announce time limits.

8. Try to handle each piece of paper only once at a time. Keeping pending will consume time to read it again.

9. Time is a valuable resource of your's as well as that of every employee. Unless you learn to manage it well, you cannot manage anything well. A fraction of time cannot be bought by a ton of gold. You can decide how to spend time. Time is man's most

precious commodity and you should have optimum utilisation of every fraction of a second.

10. Be precise. Squeeze more from your time by thinking ahead and eliminating time wasters in order to gain efficiency. Try to take time to get right details and save the time of doing it again. For example, in one of the company, the Managing Director asked his Production Controller to give exact number of 'Contact Tip' available in stock, within a hour, to obtain order of switchgears for delivery within a month. Contact Tip was critical item due to lead time involved to obtain its delivery. Counting in numbers within a hour was not possible due to its bulk stock. So the total weight of item was taken in kg. which was multiplied by number of pieces per kg. to arrive at a stock in numbers. Thus, completed the job by concept of approximation within stipulated time.
11. Do one thing at a time. Skill upgradation is essential for survival. Multi-tasking although sometimes unavoidable, is an overrated skill, which reduces the sudden impact of transfer and relocation etc. Do not attempt to do too much, in too little time. Delegate more.
12. Eliminate non-essential things and,
    (i) Spend time doing those things which are of greater value.
    (ii) Expand your work according to the available time for completion instead of being a perfectionist to consume lots of time. To **complete work in less time makes all the difference.**
13. If you find it difficult to get any **"Quiet Time"**, try to arrive at the office before anyone else, to gain uninterrupted time for planning and other tasks.
14. Continue to review and dispose. Review actual performance against each objective, to ensure desired results.

15. Set **up a future desk date file, to provide you an automatic method of bringing papers to your attention on a specific date** in the future.
16. Don't encourage 'YES' men. Eventually, they will destroy you and your vision will become blurred.
17. Be decisive. Take workable and acceptable decisions. Gather all the relevant facts. Involve other concerned people. Brief and discuss in a group to reduce ambiguity. Be committed to the decisions taken. Once decision is taken, proceed with the action to finish the job. **Ensure that every operation should be productive at all times.** For example, there is a story of Father, Son and Camel. Once a father with his son were walking down the road and a Camel crossed their way. The Son wanted to buy the Camel but his father refused. Approximately after five years, the father and his son were travelling in their horse car and the son asked his father, 'Can we buy the Camel?' In turn, father gave him the consent. The son could not control himself and asked his father; why he had not allowed to buy the camel 5 years back, when it was available at a cheap price. The father replied, "At that time our priorities were different since we were in need of money to start our own business. Now, we can afford it, as well as use it for our own business."
18. Keep the inside of your desk and files clean. **Avoid a disorderly accumulation.** Keep everything you are not working-on-immediately out of your working area and if possible, assign such jobs to others. Always tidy your desk and work area before leaving the office.
19. Tough times never last, but tough people do. Prepare and implement an action plan for each objective to be achieved.
20. **Disappointment is the difference between expectations and reality.** If you are always 'putting out fires'

ask yourself after each crisis (a) Why did it occur? (b) What can be done to prevent its recurrence? (c) How can I handle it better next time, if it does recur? Most problems are really due to absence of ideas. **If you don't like your results, change your approach!**

21. **Search your heart a number of times each day "Is what I am doing or about to do, moving me towards my objectives?"** Analyse always **"What is the most important use of my time right now?"** This will help you to focus on **'important tasks'. Measure results and not the activities.**
22. Identify areas of duplication and eliminate them. **Eliminate unproductive practices and procedures first.**
23. Identify and stop work that does not contribute directly to improve productivity, quality, value, customer satisfaction, employees benefit and profit. This will result in **'A quick hit cost saving'** by stoppage of work that makes no sense. Net **profit is a by-product of excellence, not an end in itself.**
24. Skill is not enough. It is your attitude, knowledge and self-discipline that makes the difference. **You are expected to be a quick-witted, fast-thinking and fast-adapting person with speed and accuracy in your work.**
25. Keep people around, who are smarter than you and listen to them. **Learn from the best. Try to become a man of value.** Surround yourself with positive and healthy people. Make friends who are optimists and keep a sense of perspective.
26. Decide with whom, how, when, where and why you want to spend your free time, rather than simply responding to the demands of others. It is important to have a 'family feeling' in an organisation.
27. Before leaving the office, place tomorrow's top

priority projects at the centre of your table. Put second and third priority list nearby. Distinguish between the urgent and the important. You may need to respond immediately to the urgent. **Identify and ensure continuity to mission critical areas.**

28. A manager succeeds or fails not because of what he does, but because of how much he is able to extract work from others.
29. Change for the sake of change is never good. Maintaining status quo is unhealthy for the organisation. **Both change and continuity must run simultaneously in an organisation. Ensure that the present is always brighter than the past.**
30. Empty your mind daily before retiring. Keep your mind open, clear and receptive for the next morning; so that fresh ideas blow in. There is a story in which an professor meet to the Zen master to know all about Zenism. After some discussion, the Zen master pours tea in a cup from pot for the professor. After few seconds, it started spilling and the professor shouted, "Master, master no more will go in the cup." The master replied, "Yes, like this cup your mind is overflowing with your own ideas. You must empty your mind a little to absorb new ideas." We must not be pre-occupied with own views and opinion.

The value to work on 'THINGS TO DO TODAY' is to be vigilant, so that you can identify problems and find their solutions on a day-to-day basis. Based upon your actual performance each day, you should frequently review your targets to achieve each week, fortnight, month and year. Besides, you will feel yourself more productive and secure in your job, when you have efficient and effective control on "What you do each day."

As you are aware; life by necessity is a 'DO—IT—YOURSELF', since people determine you only by productivity. The reason most people fail to achieve their goals in life is that they never set their goals in the first place. Help yourself, if you don't, no one else will.

The secret formula for success is to imagine, for a moment, that today is your last day in the present assignment and then you have to move on to a higher responsibility. At this juncture, can you analyse all your priorities, goals and aspirations? If you act accordingly, this will help you to become more focussed and committed to achieve better results every day.

The world expect results. Inaction is the other name of death. Bhagawad Gita Chapter 2 text 50 teaches us . . . . "योग: कर्मसु कौशलम्" and therefore, we have to strive to be skillful in each and everything we do.

SPECIMEN.

Things to do ... Today **Date....................**

TO DO

S.No.	Description	Whom to Contact	Remarks

TO CONTACT

Time	Person/Place/Phone

CONTINUING ATTENTION

S.No.	*Description*	*Status*

TO FOLLOW UP (PRIORITIES)

Subject	*Priority*

3

Desires and Dreams—Always Come True

"Either live with glorious victory or die with fame."

—*Shakespeare.*

What are your dreams? What are your objectives? What is your target? Why do some people succeed while others do not?

Remember! an aimless life is always a miserable life. The quality of your life depends upon the quality of your aims. Achievers possess a number of qualities apart from the fact that they are dreamers. They develop self-confidence, self-esteem and discipline. Life can be as big, as you dream it to be! A dream is first conceived as an idea in someone's mind to achieve. **DREAMS are visions of the future. DESIRE is the motivation to accomplish any dream. Achievers have dreams of life and they have strong desire to convert their dreams into a reality.** Your success and happiness lie in you. Decide your dreams. **An individual is a product of his thoughts. A person without imagination is like a bird without wings. If you want to achieve great things, you need to have a great dream. You become what you think.** If you advance confidently in the direction of your dreams and endeavour to live the life as you imagined, you will meet with success as desired. When you have dreams to nurture and develop them, you become successful. You must turn your dreams into goals. Pursue your dreams to get things rolling from a standing stop. The difficulty lies not so much in developing new ideas but in escaping from the old ones.

On this earth, every one of us gets what he deserves. You are much better than what you think you are. Fill your life with positive images and thoughts. Create a positive vision for your future. Without vision you will waste your minutes, hours, days, weeks, months and even years with no purpose and the time spent will bear no fruits. Remember! "Your mind is like a parachute. It only works, when it is open." Keep your mind open and see your future as very promising. Always look for more ways and things to do. Compete with the best. Set your goals high then exceed them! Surround yourself with persons with large, progressive ideas. Use big, bright, cheerful words. Use words that promise victory, hope, happiness and pleasure. See what can be done; not just what it is. As rightly said by Bernard Shaw: "You see things and say: Why? But I dream of things that never were and say: Why not?" Practice adding values to things, people and yourself. Focus your attention on big objectives. Decide the situation which will get you, where you want to go. Remember! it pays in every way to think big. Make a supreme effort to put only the positive thoughts in your memory bank. Doing always right is a basic practical rule for success. Make sure that what you plan to do—is right. Analyse all factors. Then be decisive and do it. Ideas alone will not bring success. Ideas have values only when you act upon them. Dream big and never lose sight of your dreams but keep them alive. The difference between a successful person and a very successful person is their size of dreams. The choice is yours.

Everything begins with a thought. Thinking turns experience into insight. What we think determines who we are. Who are we determines what we do. The actions of men are the best interpreters of their thoughts. Clarity of thought results in firmness of decisions. Our thoughts determine our destiny. People who reach to the top think differently from others. We can change the way we think. Thus change your thinking to change your life.

Everyone thinks of changing the world but no one thinks of changing himself. Remember! good thoughts and good actions will certainly produce good results. Therefore, eliminate negative thinking from your mind.

The person with a plan and picture will go after thoughts that add value to their thinking. Creativity comes from trust. What do we want to accomplish? Why do I like this idea? What is the value of this idea? What happens, if I don't do it at all? How to break out of your limitations to explore ideas and options to experience creative breakthrough? Align your resources with your objectives. Be decisive. The man who is prepared has his battle half fought. Until thought is linked with purpose, there is no intelligent accomplishment. Well begun is half the work done!

When you attain some of your objectives, your confidence will grow in your own abilities and you will begin to aim higher to convert your dreams into reality. The vision continues to expand when you attain objectives. The destiny is getting shaped and destinations are being reached. Inspire others to go for their future dreams. Encourage people to dream—big dreams. Having achieved those dreams, let them go to dream bigger dreams. Then support people to make their dreams come true. Remember! Henry Ford has said: "My best friend is the one who brings out the best in me." Your success is our mission.

Good mind, good find. You are what you think you are. Upgrade your thinking to think like important people. It helps you to think important, when you look important. How you look on the outside depends upon how you feel on the inside. Concentrate on your positive points. A wise man will be master of his mind to think: "I can do better."

There is scope for doing everything better. When you think of better, the ways to do better will appear in your creative thinking power." Think and dream creatively. Thinking is the bridge that links where you are to where you want to be. Your desire to add value to others will result in added value to you. Give to the world the best you have and the best will come back to you. When you are good to others, you are best to yourself. Think, prepare, plan and take action. The joy is in creating, not in maintaining. The individual should think with widest possible vision to cover large areas, enliven with new ideas with freedom of thought in total perspective. Never underestimate yourself since the pride and respect is largely one's own creation. People with clear thought, good desire, with a definite goal—achieve victory. Firm determination, perseverance, efforts, hard work and self-confidence, inspire and enthuse individuals to reach new heights in every field. The capacity to achieve will come itself by good intentions and positive attitude. Mental strength is a cultivated habit which together with discipline helps in positive thinking to reach the destination. Enthusiasm is an invaluable asset that helps in building dreams with happiness and satisfaction. You are energetic; looking for challenges, excitement and a bright future. "You can make your life grow any way you want, so it is important that you make the right choice. In this age of discovery and dreams, anyone and everyone can dream not only for a good future for themselves, but also a good future for their Organisation, Nation and the entire Humanity. Life is not just what it is, but life is what you make out of it. The key to happiness is having dreams. The key to success is making dreams come true.

4

The Art of Developing Self-Confidence—A Step to Success

The success of a person depends mostly on his self-confidence. Self-development is a continuous process right from birth till the end of life and every individual has to continually update his knowledge, competency and skills to maintain his effectiveness and self-confidence.

The following steps would help in building self-confidence which is a pre-requisite to success:

(i) Do not be afraid of difficulties and you should face them with courage and confidence. Develop the habit of initiative to face the issue. You should know that victory depends upon strong will power and enthusiasm.

(ii) Inspire yourself and others around you—it multiplies your achievements.

(iii) Adopt an empathic attitude towards others—it works like magic.

(iv) Try to get rid of unnecessary guilt feelings. Undertake your work with full potential.

(v) Control pessimistic thoughts—they invariably spoil you. Substitute a positive emotion for every negative thought infused in you by someone including yourself.

(vi) Take right decisions quickly. Learn to be optimistic.

Do not leave the work, when you have decided to start. I would like to cite an example "teach him to have faith in his own self and his ideas" . . .

Abraham Lincoln, the 16th President of the United States of America (1861-65) once wrote a letter to the Headmaster of his son's school. Here are a few extracts from that letter:

"He will have to learn, I know, that all men are not just, all men are not true. But teach him also that for every scoundrel, there is a hero; that for every selfish man, there is a dedicated leaders . . ."

"Teach him that for every enemy, there is a friend. It will take time, I know; but teach him, if you can, that a dollar earned is of far more value than five found . . . . Teach him to learn to lose and also to enjoy winning. Teach him that it is far more honourable to lose than to cheat. . . . Teach him that nothing is accomplished without hard and sincere work. Steer him away from envy, if you can."

"Teach him the secret of quiet laughter, quite time for himself. Teach him, if you can, the wonder of books . . . but also give him quiet time for pondering over the eternal mystery of birds in the sky, bees in the sun, and flowers on a green hill-side."

"Teach him early in life to have faith in his own self and his ideas, even if everyone tells him they are wrong. . . Try to give strength and wisdom to my son not to follow the crowd when everyone is getting on the bandwagon. Teach him to listen to all men but teach him also to filter all he hears on a screen of truth and take only the good that comes through . . ."

"Teach him, if you can, how to laugh when he is sad . . . Teach him there is no shame in committing mistakes, but teach him also that it is a sin not to own mistakes. . . Teach him to stand for the right and fight hard if he thinks he's right. . . ."

"Treat him gently; but do not cuddle him because only the test of fire makes fine steel. Let him have the courage to be impatient . . . let him have the patience to be brave. Teach him always to have sublime faith in himself, because then he will always have sublime faith in mankind. . . ."

"Teach him to scoff at cynics and to beware of too much sweetness. . . . Teach him to sell his brawn and brain to the highest bidders; but never to put a price tag on his heart and soul."

"This is a big order; but see what you can do. . . . He is such a fine little fellow, my son."

(vii) Decide the goals first, then go for the sequence of each operation into functional objectives to achieve these goals. Take at least one step everyday for fulfilling one of those goals.

(viii) Start afresh with a determination everyday to do the jobs better than before and adopt new techniques.

(ix) Dedicate your life for self-improvement and continuous learning. Learn how to improve yourself and work with others. Apportion your time to do your best.

(x) Develop trust—you only get it, if you give it.

(xi) Conduct in such a way that others develop confidence in you and let them feel that you will keep your promises.

(xii) Delegate yourself in **Identified Key Result Areas**. Do not try to monopolise.

(xiii) Do not be in a hurry for gaining appreciation and respect.

(xiv) See the victory in front of your eyes and concentrate your mind to achieve the goals.

Real development takes place when the individual realises the need to modify his behaviour, change his attitude, develop new skills, improve his performance and prepare himself for some superior role. The skills in influencing and convincing people, getting along with others, presenting ideas convincingly, are the invaluable signs of development. **While the weak wait for opportunities, the strong create opportunities.**

There is a story from Ramayana that Hanumanji did not know his potential. When there was necessity to send some one, to cross Hind Mahasagar (Indian Ocean) in search of Sita at Sri Lanka; everyone were participating in discussion regarding their capabilities but Hanumanji was completely silent. When, Jamvbant motivated Hanumanji that he has the potential, courage and capability to cross the sea and fly over to Sri Lanka; he was encouraged and inspired. With the confidence that he can do it; the results delivered by Hanumanji is the history in itself. Believe it, that you are much capable than what you think you are.

"If you have no confidence in self, you are twice defeated in the race of life. With confidence, you have won even before you have started."

—Marcus Garvey

5

How to Stay Ahead than Your Competitors?

"It is important to know yourself well; and your competitor even better. Engage your competitor in your area of strength, not the other way round."

"The only definition of business purpose is to create the customers." Keeping an eye on your competition will help you to: avoid surprises, separate rumour from reality, identify threats to your market position and to analyse new opportunities in market place. Better to prepare the master list of the competitors name with their strengths and weaknesses.

You may use the competitive intelligence system for collecting, analysing, evaluating and managing informations that affects an organisation's plans, decisions, over-all operations and performance to create a competitive advantage. This provide the details of risk/warning to business as well as to identify the new markets. Besides, it furnish the track of the competitors plan and their customers which are pre-requisite for survival of your business to counter against the competitors. You need to know what your competitors are doing, what resources they intend to use and how you can counter their move. A clearer perspective of the competitors can keep you out-of-trouble because you know, what to do before you get into trouble. Some competitive tactics are given below as guidelines:

(1) In today's world everyone is behind everyone's business. Never underestimate your competitors as they may be most important enemy in the market place. In fact, you are safer provided you reasonably overestimate them. Gather informations on what your competitors are planning and take corrective measures.

(2) **"Better a hundred enemies outside the family than one inside."** Identify and remove the inside enemy, who can be the source to leak-out the top secrets of your organisation to your competitors. The historical example is *Ramayana* in which king Ravana not only lost the battle of Sri Lanka but also his life on account of leakage of the top secrets by his brother Vibhisana.

(3) Avoid a competitors strength and exploit their weakness to promote your business.

(4) Never build your programme around your competitors mistakes since they may correct and improve them within short time.

(5) Foresee the actions of your competitors. Be careful about your big competitors. Slowly build your business and momentum in market place, where you are less visible. For example, Indian companies persue global ambitions are competing across foreign markets. Bajaj Auto competes with Honda in India as well as against the Japanese giants in Asia. Ranbaxy Laboratories Ltd. competes Merck not only in India but also in US, Europe and China. Infosys face competition with IBM in India as well as in US.

(6) Formulate plans for action rather than randomly reacting to situation. It is better to act, don't react.

(7) If a bigger competitor is about to attack, you must attack first to face reality about size and force. If you don't, you will be over-run quickly and decisively.

(8) Competitions are won first in mind. *Bhagawad Gita*

Chapter 6, Text 6 says:

बन्धुरात्मात्मनस्तस्य येनात्मैवात्मना जितः।
अनात्मनस्तु शत्रुत्वे वर्तेतात्मैव शत्रुवत्॥

"For him who has conquered the mind, the mind is his best of friends; but for one who has failed to do so, his mind will remain the greatest enemy."

जो जीत लेता आपको, वह बन्धु अपना आप ही।
जाना न अपने को स्वयं, रिपु सी करे रिपुता वही॥

Steady the battlefield before the battle begins. Crush your smaller competitors as soon as possible. In war, the GENERALS have an important maxim about being attacked. You must move even against your smaller competitors as soon as possible to avoid them develop their legitimacy and momentum in market. *Bhagawad Gita*, Chapter 11, Text 34 says:

मया हतांस्त्वं जहि मा व्यतिष्ठा,
युध्यस्व जेतासि रणे सपत्नान्।

"Therefore, kill your enemies and do not be disturbed. Simply fight and you will vanquish your enemies in battle."

अब मार इन सब शत्रुओं को, वीरवर! व्याकुल न हो।
कर युद्ध रण में, शत्रुओं को पार्थ जीतेगा अहो॥

(9) Aim at the competitors strength and his entire defence must collapse. Spot the weakness in competitors and aim all actions at it, until he fails. Be certain to defeat the competitors strength; otherwise you will be defeated in turn.

(10) Anticipate market place changes to tap new business opportunities. Analyse—"Do we have a 'significant product difference? Do we have unique and effective advantage in distribution?"

(11) You want to eliminate your competitors. Knowledge is the key to effectively overpower a competitors

profit place. You need to know your own and your competitors comparative costs and profitability-by accounts, by classification of products and by geographical distribution. You must have a clear cost advantage before attacking; otherwise, competitors can counter with price cuts that makes your attack insensible. For example, in FMCG sector Procter & Gamble sharply slashed their price of detergents since November, 2003 to increase their market share in India but Hindustan Lever Ltd. counter with the price cuts of their detergents. Can it really win this war? No one could win till August, 2004.

(12) Learn about new technologies, products and process. You have to mix and match technologies suitable to grow and evolve your business. You should actually see, how your solutions will work before you begin to implement. Even during the implementation, you can make modifications to respond new business demands or to counter the competition.

(13) The best way to predict the future is to create it. If you are losing the battle, shift the battlefield at the place, where you can take advantage of your strength. Use these tactics only as a last resort and when there are reasons to believe that the battle can be won. Complete the preparations before start of the battle. Don't go to battle unarmed but enter the battlefield fully armed to win. The only way to win, is to prepare to win. *Bhagawad Gita*, Chapter 11, Text 33 says:

तस्मात्वमुतिष्ठ यशो लभस्व,
जित्वा शत्रून् भुङ्क्ष्व राज्यं समृद्धम्।

"Therefore, get up. Prepare to fight and win glory. Conquer your enemies and enjoy a flourishing kingdom."

अतएव उठ रिपुदल विजय कर, प्राप्त कर सम्मान को।
फिर भोग इस धन धान्य से परिपूर्ण, राज्य महान् को।।

If you do what you have been doing, you will get what you

have always got. Success against odds require you to think and act differently. The above tactics have to be used properly to flourish business based upon your physical, mental and financial strength to withstand. Observe the above aspects and their variations in action around you to modify the same with your wisdom before you put into action. When you see an opportunity, pursue with great vigour. History is created when sharp minds people with an optimistic approach, a positive attitude, talent, passion, ambitions, innovative ideas with courage and determined to success come together with cutting edge technologies to achieve extraordinary lasting solutions to tomorrows problems. If you don't use these tactics, they can be used against you. "In today's competing world, it is not enough to know how to play the game properly. Sometimes, a win is possible only if you can change the rules of the game."

6

Setting Goals to Achieve the Total Organisational Objectives—Targets Boost the Morale

PART I

The successful leaders are the result of a clean, finely tuned, pre-planned approach and definite well-executed plan to achieve and excel in their areas. You have to evolve newer means and methods because you are competing in a global market.

DEFINITIONS OF A GOAL

(i) Goals are guidelines which provides direction, clarity and motivation.
(ii) Goals are mandatory and efforts become purposeful.
(iii) Goals are targets and expectations become clear.
(iv) Goals are something, the Company would like you to hit; to explore opportunities for achievement, recognition and job enrichment.

THE IMPORTANCE OF GOAL

"FIND PURPOSE, THE MEANS WILL FOLLOWS". Aimlessness is a bad habit, such drifting must not continue; without any purpose, there can be no intelligent accomplishment. Conceive a central purpose and mentally mark out a pathway to its achievement. Inject a person with the knowledge of what one wants and inspire him with energy and power to reach it.

PROCESS OF SYSTEMATIC GOAL SETTING

(i) INFORMATION: Gather and interpret its relevance and cost effectiveness.

(ii) APPRAISE: Define the situation where you are located. Identify the need, evaluating previous outcome. SWOT analysis.

(iii) SET GOALS: Where would we like to be? Problem orientation.

(iv) DEVELOP: What options or solutions are available? Identify distinctions and relationships. Anticipate future changes.

(v) REFINE: Measure qualitative and quantitative options to clarify which one is better.

(vi) DECIDE: Develop action steps. Schedule your programme. Set performance standards. Promulgate policies and procedures. Allocate resources and then organise them.

(vii) IMPLEMENT: Begin activities. Take action.

(viii) REVIEW: Compare performance with standards, analyze variance and cause of any deviations.

(ix) ADJUST: Reallocate resources. Reorganize. Resume activities and action.

NECESSITY TO TAKE RISK FOR SETTING GOALS

(i) It is necessary for survival.

(ii) It lets you control the speed and direction of change.

(iii) It makes change affordable.

(iv) You avoid the high cost and you get free publicity.

(v) Turn weakness into strength.

(vi) Do the right thing for the right reason.

(vii) Control things instead of letting them to control you.

Goals form a bridge to cross the gap between the present

and the preferred future. They also form link between policy and action plan. Goals are not wishes, but realistic and attainable for accomplishments. Goals are aimed to achieve the target.

FUNDAMENTAL QUESTIONS TO ACHIEVE THE OBJECTIVES

- Where are you today? Evaluate previous outcome.
- Where do you need to be?
- How much time you have, to get there? What options or solutions are available?
- How will you do it, if it is the competitor ; who does these things?

DESIRABLE CHARACTERISTICS OF GOALS

- Goals should be based on belief that everything is ordered to achieve the best overall results.
- A goal should be set to have higher productivity, however at the cost of other activities.
- A goal should be maintainable so that it can be revised without drastic change.
- A goal should be economic and the benefit of reaching the goal should exceed the additional cost involved.
- A goal should be legitimate and it should have official status.
- A goal should be understandable and it should be written ideally in language of the people who are required to reach it.
- A goal should be applicable and be adaptable to fit the conditions of use.
- A goal should be worthwhile by benefiting those who do the added work.
- A goal should be equitable for merit rating of individuals.
- A goal should be quantified and qualified to achieve within stipulated time.

TOTAL ORGANISATIONAL GOALS

Introduce entire working into a system, market it and force internal discipline. Objectives can be identified and formulated in all areas and they should be regularly reviewed, revised and augmented, with new objectives replacing those that have been achieved. The first step is to DRAW UP AN INVENTORY OF YOUR OBJECTIVES, wording them in a way that clarifies exactly what action you intend to take. Once your objectives have been identified and placed in order of priority, the next step is to formulate plans for their achievements.

For instance, few, out of the **TOTAL ORGANISATIONAL GOALS** are identified as under which need to be planned to achieve in a phased manner:

S. No.	*UP* ↑	*DOWN* ↓
(i)	Quality. Technology Upgradation.	Rejects / Waste/Defects.
(ii)	Productivity. Improved Process for Value Creation. Value Addition to Products. Improved Operational Efficiency.	Substandard Process. Substandard Products.
(iii)	Maximize Equipments Effectiveness and Improve Capacity Utilisation.	Setting Time.
(iv)	Autonomous Maintenance.	Equipments Breakdown. Equipments Shutdown. Equipments Stoppage.
(v)	Turnover. Development of New Market Segment.	Process Stock. Inventory.
(vi)	Profitability. Creation of Value for Shareholders, Customers, Employees and Society.	Continuous Cost.
(vii)	Optimum Use of All Available Resources and Higher Capacity Utilisation.	Losses in Material. Consumption. Losses in Power Consumption

S. No.	UP ↑	DOWN ↓
	Creativity and Innovation for Continuous Improvement with Sustainable Development. Entering New Product Segments.	Losses in Material Handling.
(viii)	Manpower Efficiency. Continue to Upgrade Skills, Knowledge and Competencies. Attract and Retain the Best Talent and Create a Talent Pool to become a Performance Driven Organisation.	Losses and Idle Hours in Manpower Engagement.
(ix)	Work Simplification (Systems Perfection).	Human Mistakes.
(x)	Standardization.	Deviation from Standards.
(xi)	Improved Safety and Hygiene.	Accidents.
(xii)	Continuous Customers Satisfaction.	Complaints.

FORMULATE PLAN TO ACHIEVE THE GOALS

TIME IS PRECIOUS and **care** should be taken to use the same which we would have taken **to spend each goal coin.** Good time planning is essential in the following areas:

(i) Where appropriate, include in your planning, a time frame for achievement of goals in a phased manner.
(ii) Make up for time loss.
(iii) Make your plans as specific as possible.
(iv) Concentrate on a limited number of tasks.

The goals should be set by involving individuals to determine their accountability and responsibility. In a competitive business, there is a sense of urgency and commitment to do it, before the competitor does it.

STEPS TO ACHIEVE THE GOALS

Your decision could crash your career even before its launch. Therefore, always think a step ahead and check your steps to achieve your goals. All of you are aware that PERFORMANCE is a combination of factors like: **(i) Goal, (ii) Standards, (iii) Feedback, (iv) Opportunity, (v) Means, (vi) Competence and (vii) Motivation.** The right goal with motive to achieve goal, opens the door for someone for superior performance.

If you wish to achieve anything big in your life, you must first set the goals. When you put up goals on paper, it takes shape and the evolution of goal begins in mind. Goal oriented people concentrate their mind on goal and begin to decide their activities to achieve the end results. Goals are like maps, which help you to reach your destination much faster. **The goals must be for improvement to make things easier, better, faster and cheaper.**

Setting goals gives people the sense of control that leads to action. Work with your staff to set their goals. Check their progress regularly. Thus you can ensure employees enthusiasm and motivation from the start to achieve the set goals—and save precious resources like time, money and energy.

The steps to achieve the goals are given below:

- Identify your strengths.
- Be positive about yourself. Have a strong reason for wanting to achieve something.
- Have a vision.
- Convert the vision into an achievable objective. Plan your priorities carefully.
- All good performance starts with the clear goals. Ensure that each person's goals are clearly defined. Make goal setting easy. Keep goals short and simple. Make goals worthwhile and challenging. Put goals in writing. See that individual's knows where they are going and what is expected as good performance needs from them. Priorities goal with organisational needs.
- Bring freshness in your thinking process.
- Analyse various views and recognise their differences.

- Try to understand views of others. Analyse what is wrong, if many disagree with your opinion. Correct yourself and don't try to do everything yourself.
- Bring out the talent in others and encourage them to find solutions to their problems.
- Encourage others working with you. Appreciate others heartily. They will be eager to reciprocate your help.
- Be friendly and polite in dealing with others. Be cheerful and enthusiastic. Show interest in all important things.
- Do not put obstruction on those who are over enthusiastic, otherwise they may lose their courage.
- People are afraid to act when they believe that once committed to a goal, they can't change their minds. Coach employees to determine the alternatives available in case of difficulties. Flexibility fosters intelligent risk taking.
- Keep anger under control. It really helps. Anger discourages initiative and damages loyalty and relationships.
- Start with a thing in which you are familiar instead of going to a completely new one.
- Make it clear that everyone has a part to play in the accomplishment to achieve the overall goals.
- Make others believe that you will not shaken their confidence in you.
- Create appropriate **"TIME CULTURE"** throughout your organisation by setting proper time standards. This will send positive signals to every employee. Take action for achieving goals and reward the results.
- Do not get discouraged by looking at those who have achieved great success. In the process of comparison, look at those who are even below us.
- Have the mind set that we are at par with everyone else and we need to improve further.
- Firmly believe that you can achieve the goals. Act to

execute and attain it.

- Keep preserving till you succeed.
- Know when to ask for help and when to involve others in your plans. Seek support. Speak out with somebody openly. Discuss the difficulties and ask for their help when essential.
- When goal achieved, celebrate success. Try to turn everyone into a winner.

WHEN TO REVISE GOALS PERIODICALLY

- Business conditions change.
- Key assumption prove wrong.
- Organizational priorities change.
- New responsibilities are added.
- Current goals are not measurable.
- Current goals are not challenging enough.

CONCLUSION

"Good thinking is wise thing, making a good plan is wiser but executing it well is the wisest." Accomplishing goals leads to self-confidence, greater risk taking and more correct action. In order to help people to establish higher goals, persuade them to stretch just a little higher first. Then ask them to gradually stretch some more until they achieve desired success in results.

The goal represents belief and plans. They indicate ambitions of management and their commitment to employees for their personal growth. Therefore, it is essential to set goal and review them periodically in close coordination to your immediate superiors to achieve the planned target. The secret of success is in constancy of purpose.

PART II

INTRODUCTION

There is a magic in thinking big! Expect and anticipate

great things to happen! Get involved! Deliberately increase your self -esteem by exercising your own influence over events. Get excited about life and its opportunities for high achievements. Think about goals and aspirations that interest you. Goals generate excitement and energy, to help focus effort; they are the avenue to effect change in your life. Write them down and prioritise them; break up each into its constituent parts and identify specific activities leading to its achievement. Imagine in your mind to attain every goal and put a time limit on its achievement. Having a specific goal and with a definite time to achieve it, is the key to success. *To try is to succeed.*

Which goals are appropriate for you in recognition of your potential for high achievement? Ideas are very powerful things and they can become your goals! If you don't know what you want, you can waste a lot of time and energy going in the wrong direction.

Take time to think! Probe your mind. You receive the greatest satisfaction from using your untapped potential to achieve goals that are set by you rather than goals that are set for you by others. Deciding what you want is often more difficult than getting what you want. You must know where you want to go, since you will work towards a goal only, if you have a goal in mind to work. Then work tirelessly to accomplish these goals.

Keep in mind this simple *PROBE* rule while formulating your goals that are:

P = Practical
R = Reasonable
O = Obtainable
B = Big
E = Exciting

Many individuals lack a few things in their attitudes like mission in life, a passion, a purpose of their talents and creativity. Without goals, life can become dull, empty and uninspiring. We all need something that moves us, that we enjoy doing. We need to feel useful.

A meaningful life is a continuous process that includes purposeful goals. If you know about your goals, the opportunities will come to enable you to carry them out. Aiming your goals gives peace of mind, clarity of thoughts, with a hope for future. It motivates you, guiding your daily decisions so that you can make the best out of unforeseeable future. The results can be reviewed, guiding your everyday actions and decisions. When you think it, you see it, you believe it, you can do it and let us try it. This kind of perspective allows you to do the right thing, at the right time, for the right reason, in the right way.

SUGGESTIONS TO HELP YOU FOCUS ON YOUR GOALS

Here are some suggestions to help you focus on your goals:

1. State your goals in an optimistic way.
2. Set a definite time to complete each goal. The deadlines also serve as wake-up call. It creates a sense of urgency and forces action. With definite time to complete, you will have that extra motivation which will help you find a way to reach them.
3. Be specific in your goals which should be clear, detailed and focussed without any doubt to accomplish.
4. Make your each goal action oriented. Update your action plan to produce results. Display targets against each objective with a column for progress achieved.
5. Make a goal board and keep it in front of you.
6. Make a game of it to take each of the steps, you plan to reach your goal.
7. Be enthusiastic to talk to other people about your goals.
8. Think positive and surround yourself with other people who are working towards goals.
9. Always think about enhancing your skills. Assess the situation at work and understand how you could

have achieved the better results.

Each one of you, by virtue of being employed in the organisation, took an unwritten oath to achieve its targets. Therefore, set your own goals. Then reinvent the meaning of achievement, performance and result everyday. Provide yourself a global platform that can put you on the fast track of success. Dare to dream, dare to try and succeed. Keep yourself nurture with winner thoughts which will add value to your willpower as well as to your personality.

Few Examples are given below:

1. "Tell me .... and I am likely to forget.
   Show me .... and I may remember.
   Involve me .... and I will understand.
   Motivate me .... and I will act."

   The most important aspect is to involve and motivate people to achieve the goals.

2. In order to attain our chosen goals, the temptations and obstacles must be overcome. For example, Hanumanji encountered three obstacles which were overcome by him, while flying across the ocean to reach Lanka in search of Sita:
   (i) MENAK PARVAT appeared as a pleasure resort in the middle of the ocean and who invited Hanumanji to rest there but he refused to rest until completion of his Lord's work.
   (ii) SURSA, the mother of Snakes obstructed way of Hanumanji and threatened to eat him. Hanumanji pleaded with her to let him go but she did not relent. Hanumanji increased the size of his body and accordingly she opened her mouth wide. Suddenly, he become small and went into Sursa's open mouth and came out before she could close mouth. Sursa was pleased to bless him for his intelligence and allowed him to go.
   (iii) During further flight, he was being pulled down into water by a mysterious force of SINIKA, who had the power to bring down creatures flying

overhead. Hanumanji mercilessly killed Sinika. Sinika stands for jealousy which can never bear the rise of others. Jealousy pulls us down and deserves to be destroyed immediately.

When our goal/work is noble, we should not hesitate to pursue it to completion. "If we rest, we rust." Success is a state of mind. Dream of success and you will be successful.

(3) Another example to get started with the most unmotivated and laziest person in the world; you take him to the middle of a deep lake, hold his head under water for few seconds and leave him. An amazing thing happens which suddenly makes him the most motivated, focussed and determined person and he immediately visualises a goal—to get another breath of air—on realising that he is under water. He visualises his future and his strong determination opens doors. This is the secret of attaining goal.

(4) The *Bhagwad Gita*, Chapter 3, text 21 says—

"यद्यदाचरति श्रेष्ठस्तत्तदेवेतरो जनः।
स यत्प्रमाणं कुरूते लोकस्तदनुवर्तते।।"

What a great man performs, is followed by others. People go by the examples set by a great man.

जो कार्य करता श्रेष्ठ जन करते वही हैं और भी।
उसके प्रमाणित-पंथ पर ही, पैर धरते हैं सभी।।

WHAT CONSTITUTES YOUR PERSONALITY

Your self-image is an integral part of your personality.

- When you give yourself a positive outlook on life, you are contributing to a positive mental attitude.
- When you change your thinking, you change your beliefs.
- When you change your beliefs, you change your expectations.
- When you change your expectations, you change

your attitude.
- When you change your attitude, you change your behaviour.
- When you change your behaviour, you change your performance.
- When you change your performance, you change your life.

All meaningful changes begin when you make the efforts to change your beliefs that you are more than what you think of yourself.

PART III

GOALS

Your goals develop from your mental pictures. Goals are desires and dreams with a definite target fixed for achieving each goal. Determine what you want. Through the repetitive thought process, the desires and dreams can become specific goals. A goal is an objective, a purpose. A goal is more than a dream since it is being acted upon. Your talent, skills and abilities should be used to plan ahead. Achievers are goal - setters. They regularly set or reset short and long term goals, establish specific time-table for their accomplishment, write-down their goals and keep them in front of their eyes for accomplishment. Take steps to achieve your goals. The essence of the goals will be the way; we consciously perceive, assess, act and react. **Set your goals high, then exceed them!**

Always stay focused to determine which of our goals were truly critical to the organisation. If there is some problem, you start wondering what has gone wrong and where? What is its economic impact? Is it aligned with the organisation's strategy? How it will satisfy stake holders? What is my level of passion, talent and energy for it? Do we have the resources?

All the best—Get started now. You have made the right decision towards your success. You are going to be successful.

Your attitude is sure to achieve your goals. Your perseverance is admirable—keep it up. Great! your goal is almost within your reach. You are well on your way to great success. Overcome obstacles. **Success starts with commitment.** Keep up the good work. Make your dreams a reality. You need to take care of the following:

(i) Define the goal. Your goal must be realistic.
(ii) Your goals should be broken down into short, medium and long range.
(iii) Keep track of daily, weekly and monthly goals.
(iv) Touch your goals everyday. Get straight to your priorities.
(v) Stick to the goals. Once you have made-up your mind to achieve certain goals, do not change your decision.
(vi) Develop a mind-set of responsible action. **A man's potential for growth is limitless.**
(vii) Periodically, you should renew goals and set new goals.
(viii) If you do not like your results, you need to change your approach.

PLANNING

Merely to dream and have no plan is just wishful thinking. A goal cannot be concrete without a plan of action. Determining a course of action and establishing a timetable for achievement are essential ingredients in planning. Planning is a vital step in achievement of goals. Consistent and persistent effort causes the result you desire. Determine your time commitment for each goal and take action.

ACTION

Good planning and judgement is useless without the courage to carry it out. All desires, dreams, goals, plans and belief may be lost without plan of action for achievement. You finalise action plan that works and a plan that can enable you to accomplish your goals. Everyone wants, success. The most difficult part of success is to believe that you can succeed. Action never occurs until you believe, you can do it. Believe, take action and succeed. Action speaks louder than words. Person may doubt what you say, but they will believe what you do. You have power of knowledge. A desire to excel and fire in the belly to achieve. You want to prove yourself and to do it on your own terms. Okay. Your time starts now. "To do the right things, Make the right decision, At the right place, With the right opportunities, At the right time, With the right technology, For the right reason, In the right way, With the right attitude." Please fasten your seat belts, to get ready to take-off. When you take a step beyond a routine or compulsory work, you are headed for excellence.

ACCOUNTABILITY

The dictionary defines accountability as "being responsible for getting something done." The returns are visible i.e. quantifiable and measurable. Without accountability, we literally cannot prove our worth. Measure return on investment or cost benefit analysis. This is a three stage process for strategy, planning and goal settings and management must achieve output in results:

(i) Defining quantifiable positive objectives.

(ii) Mechanism to measure performance against these goals.

(iii) Review comparative actual performance against each objective to ensure desired results. See to it that every operation should be productive at all times.

7

Motivation—A Self-Reliance Wish

INTRODUCTION

Motivation is the energy which fuels all activity. Even the best machine cannot function, if they do not receive energy. Performance is the result of ability multiplied by motivation. If an individual has all the abilities which are needed to do a job but is least motivated to do so, one can reasonably expect the individual to perform at a very low level. Ability includes characteristics like intelligence, skill, education, know-how, experience etc. This is called the "CAN DO" component of performance. The motivation factor is referred to as the "WILL DO" component and under it one needs desire, will, ambition, interest, dedication and involvement. We need to inspire and create enthusiasm in our entire work-force to deliver their best to achieve the "TOTAL ORGANISATIONAL GOAL".

Motivation means what makes people to work and how people perform better than others. Managers of today have a great responsibility not only for the behaviour and performance of the people at work but also their own behaviour. We have to understand the current behind the human resources which makes the human being willing to work. This leads us to motivation aspects. Motivation is an inspirational process which impels employees with unity of purpose and the need to maintain better performance with harmonious relationship among the people.

Motivation is an internal feeling which produces goal, target and behaviour. Job suitable to individual ability is motivator and factors involved are recognition, achievement, growth and advancement. It is the people at work who produce results, build the system and create a congenial climate to the growth and development of organization. The involvement participation and recognition are important aspects in motivating the work-force.

Somebody defined Managers as people who have to get more than adequate results out of inadequate resources. Motivation is one of the most important functions a manager has to carry out. One can define motivation in many ways. The industrial definition is very simple. Whenever, a person enters an organization, he can think of two levels of performance. One: the minimum he can get away with; the other: the maximum he is capable of. The difference between the two is motivation.

The maximum performance a person is capable of is very interesting. The nearer one reaches that performance level, the level goes further up and this is what really "develops" a manager.

Most of the Organisations cannot produce according to its capacity because their employees are not motivated to their work and consequently are not able to contribute properly. It is realised that motivation does not bubble from the bottom but percolates from the top to develop enthusiasm and commitment among employees.

The threat, the carrot, and the instructions are the three techniques used by managers in an earnest desire to motivate staff. Motivation is not achieved by threatening people, or bribing them, or ordering them. It is achieved by an attitude you adopt to inspire your people that will generate enthusiasm and commitment to produce results.

In one of the seminars, a Senior Manager asked me "How I would lead, if I have no authority? Would co-workers follow me voluntarily because of my good ideas, strength of character and concern for their welfare?" My answer was simple "No one has a monopoly on ideas. People who rely on rank are not true leaders. Full commitment to a task cannot be compelled but it must be inspired."

TRADITIONAL WAY OF MOTIVATION

The traditional ways, we can motivate people are very simple: The Stick and the Carrot; Fear and Money. If we tell a subordinate: "I want this to be done by this evening-otherwise please do not bother to come tomorrow." There are good chances he would do it. However, the problem is: Suppose he says, "I am not going to complete the task this evening-and I am going to come tomorrow morning. Let me see what you do." Then you have a problem- because the fear is now on your side!

I remember the time I joined my first job, almost every manager used to think about fear in a big way. The word "Gate Bandh kar dega" (the gate will be closed for you) were very effective. There was hardly a manager who would not say this at least a number of times a day! Today, the situation has changed. We realise that the use of fear has gone down. More interesting is, it has not gone down only in industry and business but it has gone down at home also! When I was small-we were three children in our house. Mother would pour milk in three mugs and announce "the milk is ready, any child that does not finish its milk in three minutes is going to get a slap"- and the milk was over. Today, thanks to family planning, lack of stamina, whatever is the reason, people have just one or two children. The mother pours milk and say, "Reghav, your milk is ready". He says, "No mom, no milk today!" Negotiations start. " Should I put some Bournvita? You want Horlicks today? Be a good boy, I shall give you Cadbury in the evening..." As you can see, the use of fear has gone down. In our times, in school and colleges, a majority of our teachers and lecturers could not teach-properly, but we were scared of them. On the streets, the police! We had no criminal background, and yet the word

"Police" created palpitations. But today, I find the fear seems to be much lower than what we were experiencing earlier and consequently to manage people by fear is very difficult.

If fear doesn't work, then of course we can use money—if the stick doesn't work, use the carrot! But money creates its own problems. The first and the most important problem is: how much money is available for giving? The easiest way of giving money is overtime. But once a person gets accustomed to overtime, then he refuses to work in "normal" time. As a worker said "Time is money, but overtime is more money!" The more money a person gets, the more he wants and the overtime keeps on increasing. **"LOVE OF MORE MONEY IS THE ROOT OF ALL EVILS."** Some day, your boss says "There is too much overtime in your department. Reduce it, eliminate it!" You go back to your department and tell people: "This has to be done, that has to be done...." Immediately they ask, "How much overtime"? You say, No overtime!" They say, "No overtime? How can it be! You want work and no overtime?" So managing-by-overtime creates its own problems and very soon you cannot manage without overtime. When money is not available for this overtime, the management goes out of the window! Since we are thinking of managing in the future- we know that money and fear will play even less important role tomorrow than they are playing today.

AREAS FOR MOTIVATION TO EMPLOYEES

Then we have to think other areas to motivate people. The following areas in an Organization would motivate employees on a sustained and long-term basis:

Review and Plan

If you are going to run a successful business, **ONE HOUR OF PLANNING IS WORTH FOUR HOURS OF IMPLEMENTATION,** so the time you spend on your business plan is most important.

The best way to get your plan together is to involve your

staff. They are the ones who, in the final analysis, determine whether the plan works or not. If you involve your staff in this review of where you have been and in the planning of where you are going, the benefits will be twofold at least: you will get plans that are attainable, but, more importantly, you will find that your staff respond enthusiastically of being involved. Having set the plans, they will feel committed. Where you have got enthusiasm and commitment, you have got motivation. Get your staff to work together on an analysis which examines the strengths, weaknesses, opportunities and threats. Concentrate on your Strength, Recognise your Weaknesses, Evaluate your Opportunity and Research your Threats. Do your **SWOT ANALYSIS.** One weak link can spell disaster for the Whole Chain. Identify your weak link that can play havoc and remove the weakness. Implement the suggestions in order of priority, assigned target dates, and incorporated into the business plan and you need to make sure to keep it alight.

Participative Management

The major factor contributing towards higher productivity is the participative management. The concept of "Workers participation in Management" in many Industries have been already implemented. Industries have adopted participative management by introducing "Quality Circles". The participative management gives a feeling to the workforce, the sense of "Involvement" and thereby the self-actualisation need is satisfied.

Share Responsibility

It is a challenge, but for most people it is particularly rewarding. Give them new responsibility and watch their motivation grow.

Share Information

Every employee is concerned about the performance of his organization. A good information sharing system would be a vital link between the management and the workforce.

The key information like planned production and the production achieved, cost of production, profitability etc. could be given to employees at all levels. The employees will feel a sense of "belongingness" to the Organization. A good information sharing system could be developed in the Organization.

Employee—Development

Every one of us is interested in improving our knowledge and skill for future career growth. Improvement of skill and knowledge for the employees, in turn helps the organization in the form of improved performance. This aspect could be covered by the following methods:

Training/retraining is an area by which the knowledge and skill of an employee could be improved considerably. Proper and suitable training scheme at various levels could be designed.

Articles of interest like cost reduction, cost control, plant performance, etc, could be published in the Company's House Magazine in order to disseminate the ideas to the workforce.

The Sense of Development is the feeling of growth. I am working here, I am growing here, I am learning something new. This is a great motivator, particularly for youngsters. Youngsters of today are very ambitious. They want to go right to the top! They don't mind if they don't reach the top in this company; they would think of another company. They must go up. To the extent they feel they are learning, they are motivated and ready to work. Whenever they feel they are stagnated, demotivation comes in.

Career Planning

Proper career planning is a positive motivation for employees. On the other hand, if an employee finds that his future is bleak, it acts as a negative motivation.

Succession Planning

Proper succession planning not only helps the

management but also helps the employees and the organization as a whole. For example, if an Organization is having only one expert welder, and no succession plan is made in advance, the problem will crop up suddenly when this welder either leaves the Organization or retires. Under a good succession planning, this sort of problems would be well tackled.

Non-financial Schemes

Most of the organisations are already having financial incentive schemes and other reward schemes. All these financial schemes are short lived and do not motivate employees on a long term basis. Non-financial schemes would have a long term effect. A few examples are given below:

Non-monetary incentive scheme for good performance of the employees could be developed. Under this scheme, every year employees who have performed good job could be given merit certificate and wide publicity could be given in the house magazine.

Similarly, the Organization may introduce a system of computerized birthday greetings for its employees. Under this Scheme, each employee get a "Birthday greeting" on his/her birthday from the computer duly signed by the Chief Executive. This system worked well as a motivating factor for the employees.

In one Organization, during the Independence day/ Republic day ceremony the flag hoisting is done by the oldest employee. This gives a feeling amongst the employee—a concern for the people irrespective of organizational hierarchy.

Sense of Identity

Once a person starts feeling that he is a part of the organization, there is no reason for creating any further motivation. That feeling itself is a motivating factor. The best example is that of a housewife. We talk of bounded labour. Has anybody seen labour more bonded than a housewife? First to get up in the morning to get milk and last to go to bed. No holidays- Sundays, festival days. Everybody says: "Extra dish is required today". So extra work. The one who works like this is not even born in that family. She was born somewhere else and brought up there for twenty odd years. One fine morning she is married and we bring her to her new house and say: "This is your house. "Very silly trick! But it works!!. Within 20 days when she talks of her house, she does not mean the house she had been for 20 years, but the house she has been for 20 days !!! And once she thinks that it is her house, we don't have to put "standing orders": This house shall be kept clean at all times. She worries about you, your children, your servants to keep it clean. As we can see, the sense of identity is a very powerful motivator.

We can see this in industry also. Take the example of TISCO. During the Janata regime, George Fernandes and Biju Patnaik suggested TISCO should be nationalized. The biggest shout came from the workers of TISCO. They said you are not going to nationalise our company. All the 70,000 workers of TISCO together do not own even 1% of the shares!

The feeling of identity is very important. How can we create this feeling ? Frankly, this is not a new problem that we are facing only in industry today. It is a very old problem-starting with religion. How do people of a religion feel that they belong to the same group? We find that this trick can be used in physical work together. People working physically together get a feeling of identity. You go to a church. As soon as the service starts, people get up, sit down, sing together. This working together creates an identity. I saw a film on Haj. Muslims from all over the world go there. Each Muslim coming from a different country has a different cultural background. But once he goes there, goes around the holy stone, he starts getting a feeling of identity. This is probably why all important Hindu temples are at the top of the hills like Tirupati, Badrinath, Kedarnath, Vaishno Devi. The reason is: people should climb together.

The collective physical work is a very powerful method of creating identity. Such identity is created by the army. Motivation is a great challenge for the army. In industry what we mean by motivation is that one gets paid for 8 hours and probably works for four hours-if you can make him work for an additional hour, we say he is motivated. In military, when we talk of motivation, we mean that the soldier must risk his life! When a commander tells a soldier to go and fight the enemy and capture the enemy post, the soldier knows the enemy is not standing with a white flag in his hand. He is sitting with a machine-gun. If he starts doing a cost/benefit analysis: what are the chances of my capturing the post, getting a medal, getting promotion and what are my chances of catching a bullet and lying horizontal forever, do you think that army has any chance? The soldier must risk his life! That is motivation ! To create that motivation through identity, the army uses some very interesting methods. First is the uniform; people wearing the same uniform, looking almost alike is one method of creating identity. Then, lot of physical work together- drill, marches. During peace time, the army is not relaxing. The soldiers are often marching with the officers. To the extent we can create this kind of physical work together, we can create identity.

In Japan, this idea used in industry is also very effective. Firstly, everybody wears the same uniform—right from the chairman to the sweeper, so that a visual identity is created. Secondly, as soon as the siren goes and the factory starts functioning, everybody gets together, stands together and sings the company anthem. In India, we have problems in people even for singing the national anthem. If you ask somebody, "Why don't you sing?" he will say, "With my voice, how can I sing? "But if you start an arati of God, he will join. Why? The God is his. The nation is still on probation. We have not "confirmed" it. In Japan, people are ready to sing the company anthem-so identity with the company is already established. The third thing they do: as soon as the company anthem is over, they do physical exercises together for three minutes. What happens? Think of a sweeper-sweeping the chairman's room. The siren blows- the chairman and the sweeper stand together, sing the company anthem, do physical exercises together. The sweeper thinks: "This Chairman, I don't know how many levels he is above me. But he is still a part of my team; we have the same uniform, sing the same song and do the same exercises.

Sense of Importance

Let us look at the Sense of Importance: Let me go back home. Every wife feels she is very important. Without her, the house is going to fall! In the first or second year after marriage, she occasionally goes to the maternal place; but thereafter she does not want to go out.

How does the boss get work done from somebody? He takes him aside and says, " I don't want to give this work to anybody else. You are the chap to do it!" What it really means is that you are the only stupid chap who will work 14 hours a day and complete it. But immediately it created the motivation. So the feeling of importance is vital.

"Many people ask me: "How do you recognize sick units? Do you study the balance sheets?" I say: I don't believe balance sheets. I go to factory. I see the pipes and drums are leaking, cement in the open getting spoiled. I ask the worker: "What is happening?" He says, "Nobody is bothered!" I say, "Why don't you tell your boss?" He says, "My supervisor! Oh! That poor chap can't do anything!" I say, "Why don't you tell your Manager." He says, "He also can't do anything." Everybody is powerless. Wherever there is a feeling of powerlessness, you can't get motivation. Where people feel that they have power, they can do something. They get motivation due to a very important factor that is a sense of power. Wherever people have sense of power, they are motivated and they do the work.

Reward Adequately

Most people believe that 'money' is the most important component of motivation in the work place. Interestingly enough, it is not; once a person receives income sufficient to provide the necessities of life, extra money does not have a strong motivational effect. Sure, it is always welcomed, but it does not generate any deep, continuing enthusiasm or commitment. Therefore, you have got to pay the right price for the people you need. When your people perform well, find different special ways of rewarding them. You have to show that you have thought about your staff carefully. One of the best things you can ever do is to write a letter of appreciation just to say a simple and sincere thanks. This is the kind of reward a recipient will treasure and keep with other special mementos. When your staff has demonstrated ability in one work, reward them by giving them another challenge.

Reward is critical in motivating people for achievement. It does not matter how much you pay them, but how inventive you are in finding ways of making your appreciation of their efforts matters much.

Recognise Achievements

REAL BEAUTY IS THE BEAUTY OF SOUL. At first glance, it is easy to confuse reward and recognition, but both are different. When someone does a job well, the reward is what they get personally; the recognition is what they get publicly. Recognition is a vitally important factor, and your role is to ensure that the rest of the team, the company get to hear about your people when they do something well. You will need to work at it, but what you will get back in terms of enthusiasm and commitment will make it worthwhile. HAPPINESS IS NOT PERFECT UNTIL IT IS SHARED.

Respect the Staff

Remember that your people do not own the business or have as much at stake as you have. When it is all said and done to them it is a job. Establish conditions that generate a high level of motivation.

Too often, this aspect is forgotten and the boss expects staff to live, breathe, eat and sleep over the job just as they do. The staff may do so for a while, but they will not do it forever. Respecting your staff as an individual means realising that they have a life of their own to lead, probably a family and interests that they have to balance with the demands of the job. You become proficient in respecting your staff as individual, only if you work on it.

If you respect your staff, it increases the chances that they will like working with you and your company, and this is a part of the enthusiasm and commitment that are essential for motivation.

Report Progress

Involve your staff in periodical performance meeting to review and plan and it seems logical that you ought to let them know how the company is going in terms of those plans. Normally, managers do not share the successes and failure with staff. Nothing could be more distant from the truth. If your staff is really a part of the team, they will welcome the opportunity to share the victories and defeats.

Sit down with your people for doing your analysis. Decide the key indicators that they need to know and how often they need to get that information. Make sure, you discuss the information with them as soon as it is provided, for two reasons. First, to ensure that they understand it and, second, that you can get feedback. You may find out how to solve problems to achieve success. You will certainly get good ideas.

The reporting process includes keeping your staff members aware of how you feel about their performance. You should examine their progress constructively and in private. Praise good points and positively highlight areas where improvements can be made.

Empowering People

The way to ensure success through efficiency and higher productivity of the human resource is empowerment. The common point of conversation of employees, limits around frustration at work. While people may love the trade or work, they may dislike about dealing with people and systems. The topics centre around lack of support, problems with a boss or subordinate, seemingly irrational changes in priorities, infighting, politicking, and so on. Not all, but a few are able to make remarkable contributions. These few are known as empowered ones in the midst of bureaucratic domination.

The empowerment refers to a process in which a manager may empower subordinate managers by sharing resources with them, allowing them to participate in the decision making process and by giving them access to relevant and important information.

The individual perceptions of low levels of self-efficacy can be raised by empowering employees such as:

1. Helping employees to achieve job mastery by giving them training, coaching and guided experience.
2. Allowing them to observe individuals, who already perform successfully on the job.
3. Giving praise, encouragement and verbal feedback, to raise self confidence.
4. Providing them less of stress and anxiety through better job, task assistance and honest caring.

When Managers use these approaches, employees begin believing that they are competent and valued, that their jobs have meaning and impact and that they have opportunities to use their talents.

The process of empowerment is for success in the days to come. If people are empowered, the employees own the organisation, discharge their duties effectively, derive satisfaction from the job, then organisations record higher levels of profitability, sustainability and growth.

Few important parameters for individual as well as the organisation growth are as follows:

* Trust your people but track their performance through financial parameters.
* Empower managers to run the organisation, but decide about the future personally.
* Recounting managers with motivational abilities who alone can inspire workers.

In the absence of empowering people, the employees lack commitment, members fail to share the organisation's goals or employees are fearful or retribution if they take the initiative.

THE ART OF MOTIVATION

The secret to motivation is to learn how to influence people. Once you understand this, you are in a better position in attaining the results that you and your organization want. Here are a few tips to be a better motivator, Quote:

(i) If you have no idea what motivates a certain individual, just ask.
(ii) Learn what are the needs of your staff and help to fulfil them.
(iii) Remember that making work as a fun is not the same as making work easy. Ensure that the staff knows their roles and their importance.
(iv) Keep work as stimulating and varied as possible, allow staff to use and increase their expertise.
(v) Keep the number of supervisors and the level of supervision as low as possible.
(vi) Always remember that different people have different motivations.
(vii) Learn to differentiate between personal and work problems.
(viii) Foster team spirit through inter-team competitions.
(ix) When things go wrong, review both your motivations as well as that of your staff.
(x) Point out errors but be objective in your criticism.
(xi) Keep staff informed to policy changes or new directives immediately as uncertainties or undue delay can cause dissent.
(xii) Seek the views of your staff on decisions that affect them.
(xiii) Be wary of office politics, and do not let yourself be part of it. Form your own opinions.
(xiv) Praise work that is done well, even if not all the targets are met.
(xv) Root out and eliminate causes of repeated complaints.

(xvi) Explain reasons for unpopular decisions you have to make.
(xvii) Welcome ideas from all levels of staff.
(xviii) Set targets that are high, yet attainable.
Unquote: Extract from Essential Manager's Manual-Today's Manager

CONCLUSION

The motivation referred to above are simple but effective in increasing your employees motivation and to produce the end results, particularly when you are sure that the fear and money are not working or may not work for long. After all, we know sacking a subordinate is becoming a full time task-and the chances are fifty-fifty that who will go! In that situation, it is not worth trying to use fear on the subordinates. Using money works in the short term, but in the long term, it causes a problem. So, when fear and money are out, the above motivators become vital and this is the way we can keep on motivating a group of people. These areas once attended will bring spontaneous improvement in the performance of the employees. There may be more areas which may vary from Organization to Organization.

PART II

MOTIVATION—A SERMON AT A GATHERING

Ladies & Gentlemen,

It gives me immense pleasure to welcome you all to this august audience. We preferred our people to be charged-up, inspired and motivated. Therefore, the participation in this **management development programme** becomes essential to **discover the secret of success and adding values to our people who** will ultimately add values and success to our organisation. **We need to turn our weaknesses to strength and help our people to take on more responsibilities. We need to remove the barriers to our productivity and enhance**

mutual respect, team spirit and team work.

भुला दे अपनी हस्ती को, अगर कुछ मर्तबा चाहे।
कि दाना खाक में मिल कर, गुलोगुलजार होता है।।

One who wishes to achieve something has to forgo his self-existence similar to the seeds which gets destroyed to convert into a beautiful garden.

Why is it that your boss tells you to — **"be smart", "be innovative"** and **"think big"?** Simply, so that you can achieve targets and project higher goals for the future. What happens if you don't? You may probably get sidelined or loose your job. The choice is entirely yours. Similarly, learning is not a matter of choice, but **it need to evolve according to business needs. "SURVIVAL OF THE FITTEST"** is the universal law. **A learning organisation is the only economically sustainable organisation. Every learning needs the ability to accept, what can be done differently and better than previous success. Nothing lasts forever. Knowledge today has an expiry date like medicines and everyone of us must learn the latest practices internationally, if we have to deal with new challenges and continue to improve our position. This calls for a humble mind-set, which is open to learning.** You need to ask the simple questions like.

- Why do you get your vehicle serviced periodically?
- Why do sportsmen practice constantly?

The challenges of working in highly competitive globalised business environment demands that all members of an organisation are individually and collectively top performers and effective achievers. We believe that only enlightened, committed, motivated, happy and healthy individuals are the core of a successful organisation.

As all of you are aware, the successful organisation is one that grows at a rapid pace even under economic slowdown and difficult times. Indian family business have come under a cloud in the era of liberalisation. TODAY INHERITING A BUSINESS IS NOT A "**BED OF ROSES**". Indian business is going to fly into severe turbulence. You need to fasten your seat belts tight. The principal forces that have compelled change in Indian companies everywhere are globalisation, deregulation and new technologies etc. which demands competence. **What is competence? Competence means to be suitable and fittest in knowledge, will and skills**. This reflects the individual's ability to respond to demands placed on them of efficient work performance. The questions arise.

- How to predict new challenges?
- How to control new challenges?
- Are we fully prepared and equipped to face global competition?
- How to glue the loyalty of our employees to our company?
- How to stop the out flow of talented employees from our Company?

We must now focus on learning—How to rapidly invent our business and transform our organisation. Learning together by employees brings about fellowship, mutual understanding, team spirit and emotional integration which creates synergy amongst members of the organisation. Good ideas and innovations are driven into existence by courageous patience. Courage and self-respect are basic ingredients which unleash the energy essentially required for achieving excellence. The best way to treat the future is to invent it. Therefore, the necessity is not "JUST TO IMPROVE.... BUT TO INVENT". There are million ways to invent for improving our quality, productivity, efficiency, effectiveness, profitability and turnover etc. for which we need to use "COLLECTIVE WISDOM". Healthy competition keeps our motivation and energy level high. The collective wisdom and shared endeavour brings prosperity which controls emotions, feelings of individuals and enhance creativity for innovation. The WORKING TOGETHER works to achieve the COMMON GOALS by the devotion and efforts of every employee, which results into growth of the organisation. We need to continuously enrich self-confidence, knowledge and skills of our people by providing them facilities for exchange of ideas, opinions and informations.

Have goal(s) every morning to be achieved at the end of previous day, taking into account, obstacles and unforeseen delay that may come in our way to achieve our daily goal(s). My confidence in MANAGEMENT EDUCATION and to set future has gone stronger because one cannot work without the other. We love competition since competition is always healthy. It is like sports. **Competition makes you better and firm.** If you do not have someone to push you, you get wiped-out one day. When you fail to achieve the target, you have to analyse why it did not work or how you can make it better? **Greater success comes only to those who do not confine their thinking to a defined mould but DO THINGS DIFFERENTLY.**

कुछ लोग थे जो वक्त के सांचे में ढ़ल गये।
कुछ लोग थे जो वक्त के सांचे बदल गये।

We have to respond fast to changes. What we have achieved in last ten years can be tried to be done in a year now. What we have achieved in previous year can be tried to be done now in a month. This is because the response today is different as well as very fast. Moreover, our resources, experience and skills have improved considerably as compared to past. **We also have a top notch Management Education system** for the higher level. If we can't leverage on this asset, we will miss a crucial life time opportunity. **We need to set example for the future and go ahead with continuous improvement. Seeing is believing. It is our role to understand minds of our people and to inspire, motivate and create enthusiasm in our entire work-force to deliver their best to the organisation.** You as a leader has to find new avenues for motivation, growth and prosperity. **In order to translate our business strategies into results, we need to equip with techniques to improve our skills, performance and attitude.** You are aware that **TIME SAVED IS TIME**

EARNED AND TIME EARNED IS BUSINESS MULTIPLIED.

इन्सान, खो के वक्त को पाता नहीं कभी।
जो दम गुजर गया है वो आता नहीं कभी।

We are all potential learners, capable of growing and recreating ourselves through knowledge and experience. Learning provides the skills, insights and competence to perform well at work.

Even more important aspect is that learning enables people to adapt and grow in their jobs, becoming better problem-solvers, more creative thinkers, more confident people, and more proficient workers. As an individual becomes more knowledgeable, he or she becomes a better and valuable employee.

Within the business setting, a learning institution is company that constantly encourages and nurtures education. The task of learning, whether by an individual or by an institution, entails the acquisition of new competencies like (i) Ability to learn, (ii) Techno-knowledge, (iii) People skills, (iv) Emotional literacy, (v) Intuitive abilities and (vi) Personal management etc.

The ambitious people are concerned with excellence, competition and making an impact in their field. They accept responsibilities with important assignments and constantly manage time efficiency to achieve the targets effectively.

KNOWLEDGE IS POWER, IF WELL MANAGED. Efficient knowledge management can provide maximum return on investments. We need to bring out the best in these people. Just as water needs various levels to flow, these people need different challenges which help them grow personally as well as professionally. They need to enumerate their goals, short term or long term, as clearly and specifically as possible. They achieve clarity with respect to their goals, objectives, action plans and facilitate the process of identification on alternative strategies to achieve these goals. They should set a realistic time frame to achieve these goals.

They are high speed, competitive, aggressive, anxious and impatient to succeed in their set objectives.

It gives me a sense of satisfaction to highlight that you need to learn from past, live for today and plan for a better tomorrow. **Tough times don't last but tough people do.** You need to do your job so well that everyone says — **"Here lived a man who did his job so best as if god almighty called him at this particular moment in history to do it". "SPIRIT OF CHALLENGE" demands speed of response and new values surpassing expectations in our quality and productivity at a competitive cost in addition to our turnover and profitability.** We must strive our entire work-force to work—together as one, aiming at our common goals. **The employees at all levels needs to be inspired by the super-ordinate goals as well as the spirit of excellence for making a significant and enduring contribution as the SUPER ACHIEVERS to the organisation.**

उद्योगिनम् सिंह पुरूषो, मुपेति लक्ष्य।
देवे न देवे, इति कापुरूषा वदन्ती।।

The biggest fear is the fear of unknown and the future is unknown. Each one of you need to take care of yourself since no one else will take this responsibility. We wish to develop our people differently, to deliver the best results at quicker speed and lesser cost even under more constraints. This is essential since organisation needs people and people needs organisation. **Enjoy success whenever you have succeeded which keeps you emotionally charged.** Before I conclude, I would like to take this opportunity to thank all those who are present here for their continued support in success of our organisation and patience hearing to plan achieving the excellence in future for turnaround of the company.

PART III

SUGGESTIONS

What are your life's ambitions? Are you prepared to hit the road of success? What are your dreams and ambitions? How to get what you want? How to position yourself ahead of the others?

Believe it or not but growth is life which is possible only by motivation. Therefore, motivate people to dream, make them believe in their dreams and enable them to fulfil their dreams. Mere dreaming without action is useless. A vision without action is merely a dream **but vision with action can change the entire results. Drive people towards higher level** of efforts. **You will be surprised to see how fast motivated people can run. Motivation is a motive for acting.** We are constantly looking for ways that can help people to work more effectively. What is the key that can really unlock the potential of each one of our employees?

You may use following suggestions to motivate your employees:

1. **Create a need.** 'You can lead a horse to water but you can't make it drink unless you create a need.'
2. Develop a **sense of personal responsibility.**
3. Create and **maintain interest.** People like to be involved and people also need to be stimulated.
4. Encourage people to ask questions of interest. Besides, **give** people examples or illustrations or **information in meetings.**
5. **Give recognition, encouragement and approval.** The greatest need of every human being is the need for **appreciation.**
6. **Foster competition.**
7. **Get excited to start** process and actions for doing the job.
8. **Establish long term objectives.**

9. See the value of internal motives. People have loyalty to their organisation that helps them to accomplish things which are important in their personal as well as professional lives.
10. Intensify interpersonal relationship to make people comfortable talking to other departments to solve the problems.
11. Give people choice to fulfil their responsibility.

The constant optimum load on people always brings out the best in them through energy, example and effectiveness and make them efficient and effective by right motivation and appreciation. There are only two categories of people in this world; first those who 'Can do it' and second who 'Have done it'. It is really important to motivate people from 'Can do it' to 'Have done it', so that their dreams are converted into reality.

8

Communication—A Ready Reckoner to Success

PART I

THE ART OF COMMUNICATION

IT IS NOT WHAT YOU SAY, BUT HOW YOU SAY, THAT MATTERS. COMMUNICATION IS AN ART AND LIKE EVERY ART, IT IS IMPROVED BY EXPERIENCE AND PATIENCE. People, who are gentle in social conversations forge valuable personal ties in their BUSINESS and their RELATIONSHIPS. Effective communication helps to obtain better support and willing involvement of team members. The performance barriers can be removed by increased transparency.

PROCESS OF COMMUNICATION

Communication is a very difficult function for managers for the simple reason that everybody assumes that he is a better communicator than others.

I myself have been talking about communication for the last 28 years and suddenly I found I am also not a very good communicator. Just the other day, I read a very good article on communication. While I was reading an article, I underlined several important points. Since it was a good article, I thought of getting it cyclostyled. I told my secretary to make stencils of the article omitting the underlining. Do you know what he did? He omitted all the underlined words. When I looked at the stencils, I said, "What have you done? The stencils don't make any sense?" He said, "I know that. I thought you are preparing an exercise in communication." I said, "I asked you to omit the underlining." He said, "Underlining? I thought you asked me to omit the underlined!"

This is the problem we face every time. So let us look at the process of communication to understand where communication goes wrong. Firstly, communication is essentially a transmission of ideas. The simple method to ensure correct communication is to get the feedback.

However, asking people to give feedback is not easy. One can ask the subordinate to give feedback. How do you ask your boss? "Boss, have you understood me? Can you tell me what did I say?" Very offensive-even to a colleague. In fact, even though a subordinate may give the feedback, he may feel a bit upset. Consequently, asking feedback, although a very effective way of avoiding wrong communication, is not always very practical. So the best thing for us to do is to ask how do we handle the process so that the communication we make-goes through without distortion-without getting misunderstood.

SIMPLE COMMUNICATION—EASY TO UNDERSTAND

The first step in communication is, putting ideas into words. We have a cultural problem. In India, scholarship was always associated with not being understood by the "people". In good old days, all pandits used to talk in Sanskrit which very few could understand. So everybody felt that not understanding by somebody means that somebody is a great scholar. That tradition continues and we find many people, as soon as they feel that they have become experts, start talking in a difficult language. The first thing we must understand: At least as managers, we have no business to use a language which the other person does not follow. It defeats the very purpose of communication. Think about the words, the other person can understand. This is very useful. Every communication must have the audience in mind and must make it as simple as possible.

TRANSMISSION PROBLEMS

The second step in communication is transmission. There are several problems in transmission.

Distractions

The obvious problem is distraction by noise. If I am talking and there is a loud noise, obviously people won't hear me. But loud noise is not the only problem. Even a low whisper can be a problem. In a training programme, if some participant whispers to another participant, my communication stops. Why? Because people are more interested in listening to whispers than listening to something which I am communicating. So a whisper becomes a distraction. There can be other distractions. For example, one of the important distractions is movement-people moving about when you are communicating.

Lack of Interest

The distraction is accentuated by lack of interest. If people are not interested, it is very difficult for them to concentrate on what is going on — they can be distracted by anything. After all, many people who come to training programmes are "nominated". They are "sent". It is not that they want to learn the specific topic. Unless you can make the topic relevant to them, they won't learn. The most important thing to do is to see that what we are saying regarding the topic is relevant to the participant. As long as the participant feels the messages are not applicable to him, nothing will happen. The two disasters for any programme are: at the end of the programme somebody asks, "How was the programme?" The first reaction of the participant is, "It was a nice programme. My boss should have attended it"! The another reaction "It was interesting, but theoretical. Nothing like this can work in our company". In both cases, the programme means nothing to the individual. Then he cannot keep his interest. So you have to make the programme relevant to the person concerned clarifying what he has to practice-not what somebody else has to practice. The change required in the training situation is in the participant himself. He must see in what respect he has to change himself. This we must bring to his attention.

Hostility Barrier

However, the most difficult problem in communication is the "hostility barrier". Wherever people are hostile, they will not listen. This is where your communication is likely to get misunderstood easily- this is the barrier about which we have to make the maximum effort in order to ensure that our communication goes through. Hostility is the most important impediment to effective communication.

So let us try to understand, how do we get over with this hostility. For this, I am going to use the framework of transactional analysis which is an analysis of communication. We communicate through three attitudes which are called "ego-states": Parent, Adult and Child. Parent Ego-state is essentially the traditional messages that all of us receive right from our childhood relating to what is good, what is bad, what should be done, what should not be done, what is right, what is wrong. All these messages we receive form two things in our head. One is ethics. Everybody gets messages like: "be kind to animals," "give respect to elders", "always speak the truth," "never tell a lie," "honesty is the best policy," etc. All these messages form our ethics which is quite important in our life. Unfortunately, the parents (which means not only father and mother, but grand-parents, aunts, uncles, teachers and elderly people around us) give us some other messages also—about caste, community, belief, language, state, religion. These messages also talk about good-bad, right-wrong. This is prejudice. As a child, we don't know which is ethics and which is prejudice. Consequently, we record both. Many of our reactions as we get older are dictated by these messages. These messages are many times hostile to some groups and consequently whenever a person of that group (or we think he is of that group) starts communicating with us, the hostility barrier comes up.

The second ego-state is "Adult". This is very useful for our communication purpose. Adult is essentially learning: it receives and gives information. In this process, several of our prejudices get reduced. For example, as a high-caste Hindu, I received lot of prejudices in my childhood. "Muslims are dangerous," "Harijans are dirty," "Christian are unreliable," "Punjabis are aggressive," etc. Sometimes even a favourable prejudice e.g. "Bengalis are intellectuals": when I went to Calcutta, I found that was also not true. But most of the prejudices we receive are adverse. Consequently, when we deal with the people, we get into the problem of hostility barriers. The Adult ego-state can bring the barriers down by receiving the information.

Let me take my own example. When I first went to school, there was a boy sitting next to me. I asked him, "What is your name"? He said, "Usman". I got scared ! I was told: "Muslims are dangerous!"—so I was scared of him. But within two-three days, I found he was a very nice boy—very helpful, very friendly. I have a problem: "Parent" message says: Muslims are dangerous, Usman is Muslim—so he is dangerous. My "Adult" says Usman is a very nice chap. But I can't take a U-turn. I can't say Muslims are good—and so Usman is good. What I say is: Muslims are dangerous, but Usman is an exception!

Now this is how we start in our life—trying to make exceptions. Since I was brought up with lots of Adult messages thrown at me, very soon I came to the conclusion that being good or bad, right or wrong doesn't depend on one's caste, community, language, state, religion, but it depends on the individual person. You can look at a person and evaluate him as a person, without looking at all the background. This is a very important learning. But not everybody gets this learning in every respect. So everybody has a tendency to carry at least a few prejudices about others. This becomes very important barrier in communication. We have to look at ourselves very carefully and see to what extent this barrier exists in our mind and what we can do about it. The more experience we get, the more thinking we do, better are the chances of bringing down the barriers at a fast speed.

Another problem in communication in our "Child" ego-state is our momentarily reaction. Everybody gets impulse. If you are listening to a lecture for an hour, you feel like getting up, stretching your arms and dullness which is natural. But immediately your own "Parent" and "Adult" censor your "Child". The "Parent" says, "Faculty is Guru! We can't show disrespect to Guru!" But there are some senior people sitting here. It can be bad for me, if I sleep in their presence." So you suppress the dullness. But the impulse is there. To the extent your parent and adult do not control it, the impulse comes up. One of the results of this impulse is quarrel. After all everybody knows, by quarrelling, nobody is benefitted. Two people quarrelling in an office or in a factory ultimately results in both of them losing their stature. Everybody knows this and yet it is not very easy to avoid quarrel. Whenever you get into a situation where you feel something wrong about the other person, impulsive reaction comes up. Here **"THE VALUE OF COMMONSENSE" exist. "GO TO LAW FOR A CAT AND LOOSE A COW." TWO FARMERS CLAIMED TO OWN A CERTAIN COW-WHILE ONE PULLED ITS HEAD AND OTHER PULLED ITS TAIL. THE COW WAS MILKED ULTIMATELY BY A LAWYER.**

I remember the other day, I was staying at a hill station with a friend of mine. My friend said, "Let us walk to the next door neighbour. I want to borrow his torch." While we were walking, he said, "You know, my neighbour is a very peculiar chap. I shall ask him "Can I borrow your torch?" He will ask, "What happened to your torch?" I shall tell him,

"I had a big torch, but the cells leaked-so the torch got spoiled". "He will say, "How careless." Then he will say, "Why don't you buy a new torch?" I shall say "I want to buy a new torch-but I keep on forgetting." Then he will say, "Why don't you keep a shopping list?" just then we reached the neighbour's place. My friend rang the bell, the neighbour came out and asked, "What can I do for you?" My friend said, "Look here! If you don't want to lend your torch-don't lend your torch. But whether I keep a shopping list or not is none of your business!" I told him, "Why are you fighting with him? He didn't say anything!" My friend says, "You don't know him. I know him. I know what he is thinking." Can you see what happened. The communication that did not take place in fact took place in my friend's head because of the hostility.

If you think this is very peculiar, think of yourself. Suppose the trade union leader says, "He wants to see you at 1 p.m. today." As soon as you get this message, your blood pressure starts rising. Why? As a manager you feel that union leaders are rascals. They don't want to work themselves. They don't want others to work. So your blood pressure starts rising. You know what the union leader is going to say. He is going to say, "Why don't you give overtime to Ram" He is going to get provocative. However, you decide to keep your mind cool and plan to tell him, "Look here! According to the rules of this company, according to the agreement with the union, according to the laws of the land, Ram is not entitled to overtime." Then he is going to say, "You will have to give." Still you are going to keep your mind cool and tell him, "Look here! I don't think overtime is justified." Then he will say, "If you don't give, I shall go to your boss." You are still going to keep yourself cool and tell him. "If you want to go to the boss, you can go. "This is what you want to happen. What happens in actual practice? Union leader walks in at 1 p.m. As soon as you see him, your blood pressure starts rising again. He sits down and says, "Saab, Ram..." As soon as he says "Ram", you say, "You want to go to my boss- go to my boss!" The hostility that was created in your head comes up. As long as the hostility exists, the impulse cannot be avoided and we get into communication problem.

We have to strengthen our thinking. One of the ways is to look at the problem at the end of the day and ask: the way I reacted to the person, the way I discussed and the way I negotiated, did I manage good communication? This way one can improve communication.

Feuds (Private Enmity)

There is another aspect obstruction communication: "feuds". Lot of hostility is created in organisations by feuds e.g. Production versus Marketing. Purchasing versus Production, Accounting versus Engineering. These are the feuds that go on in every organization. How do these feuds occur?

Let us take the Accounting versus Engineering feud. Perhaps, right from the time Brahma created the first engineer and the first accountant, they have been fighting. What does the engineer say about the accountant? "Here is a chap who has authority without responsibility! If something goes wrong, something is delayed, who is responsible? The engineer! Who delays it? The accountant! And basically he is a stupid chap. If he was intelligent won't he be an engineer? Why would he be an accountant?" You go to the accountant and ask him, "What do you think of the engineer? "He says, "Engineers are very difficult people. They don't know how to argue anything logically. Any question I ask, they have *a* constant response: "Technical, Technical, Technical". Just like the Indian Airlines flight delay. What is the reason? "Technical snag." What is technical snag-may be the air-hostess forgot her vanity case! Secondly, they don't understand procedures. They want to repair a machine-very costly repairs. I tell them, "Look here! Why don't you get some quotations?" You know that they say, "let me get it repaired first. I shall get the quotation afterwards!" What is the use of quotations afterwards? Thirdly, they want to give all the repair work to the same party. I better watch them carefully, otherwise they will rob the company blind". Can you see the hostile attitude: "I am OK—You are not OK".

This is responsible for a lot of problems in communication because once feuds arise in an organization, you get lot of counter-productive activity. Once I met a marketing manager, normally a tempered person, looking very happy. I said, "What happened? You are so happy today?" He said, "You know the factory boiler has burst. They are screwed up for the next two months! His enemy No. 1 is not the marketing of the competing company, but production of his own company. The marketing manager walks into production department, whispering goes around. "See he is coming for information. Don't give him any information. Even if he asks, what is the time, you say it depends." You can see with these kinds of feuds, you cannot get communication between people.

Feelings Towards Others

We must understand why the feeling comes in: "I am OK-you are not OK. I am one who makes profit for this company. Everybody else is overheads."

Let us go back to our childhood. As a small child, the big people around you are constantly commenting on you. Some of the comments are quite appreciative: fair child, lucky child (child was born, father got a promotion), intelligent child, obedient child! These are nice comments. But not all the comments are nice. Some are critical comments: Naughty child, dark child, disobedient child, unlucky child (child was born, father lost his job). Sometimes there is a very confusing message. Child was born, father lost his mother-in-law. He says lucky child, mother says unlucky child! Very confusing.

What is more important is that there are lots of comparative messages. For example, as a child you try walking at the age of 12 months and you stumble. Everybody says, "Look at this clumsy child. Look at your elder brother. (There is always some elder brother around-he may be brother, cousin, neighbour's son. He always does things better than you). He started walking at 11 months- never stopped."

When you are eating-you are hungry. You start eating with both the hands. But there is a bottle-neck. There is only one mouth. So half the food falls down. Everybody says, "Look at this dirty child! Look at your elder brother. See he never dirties his shirt. Your shirt is always dirty." Can you see what is conveyed: he is OK-you are not OK! You carry water--it spills. Everybody says, "Look at your elder brother. He never spills water. You always do."

So you start with a frame work "I am not OK. You are OK." Some people keep this attitude right through their life. They have no confidence in themselves-have an inferiority complex.

These people can be intelligent, hard working-and yet they have no confidence in themselves. I remember somebody told me a case of his classmate. They used to sit on the same bench for years. As soon as the professor started lecturing my friend would go to sleep. His friend would take down notes. My friend put a carbon paper-and he got his notes. But whenever a professor made a mistake the chap taking notes would tell my friend, "Look here! That "+" should be ".". My friend said, "I don't know what the professor is talking about". His friend said, "I shall explain it to you." He would explain. My friend would raise his hand. Professor said, "Yes. What is the problem?" He said, "Sir! There is a mistake: that "+" should be ".". Professor asked, "Why?" He explained why. In those days professors never said "Thank you". The professor corrected himself and said, "Sit down." But the whole class would look at my friend, "This chap is always sleeping. But whenever the professor makes a mistake, his hand goes up!" He got a lot of credit. He asked his friend, "Why do you want me to get the credit? Why don't you raise your hand?" He said, "No! You do it well. When the professor asks why--I forget why." Can you see the problem. The person was very intelligent, hard working, sincere--but never succeeded in his life. Because he always had a feeling that he may not do anything well.

However, not all children remain with the life position: "I am not OK- you are OK". As a child grows, it finds that while it spills water, so does Mummy; while it spills food, so does Grandpa; while it stumbles so does Grandma. So the child moves to a feeling" I am not OK- you are not OK". Thus a few children get trapped in this box for the rest of their lives. There are not very many such people in an organization, but these small numbers are great demotivators for others because they always have a feeling: "I am not good, that is why I am working here- you are also not good, that is why you came here!" This creates a problem in communication as there is no mutual respect.

Very few children get into the box "I am OK—you are OK"—which essentially means understanding the other person's viewpoint. It is the Empathy Route. Whenever there is a conflict, there are two routes available. The right-wrong, good-bad, win-lose route which invariably leads to a quarrel or the other route which leads to empathy, compromise and tolerance. This is possible, if a person asks himself the question: "If somebody is differing with me, why he is doing so? What is his way of looking at things?" Once you understand his way of looking at things, some compromise is usually possible. This is something that we have to attempt.

However, this will not happen automatically. We have to pass through the phases. The one is wisdom after the event. Whenever we get into a quarrel and consequent lack of communication, we can sit back and ask the question: Could I have avoided it and how? After sometime, we would realize that we are heading towards loss of communication in the middle of it and then we can modify ourselves and move towards an effective communication. This is mid-sight. When we can plan in advance, consider the areas where the conflict is likely to take place, try to understand the other person, listen to him, then we acquire the foresight. For every person, this is a learning experience. If he gets into the frame of mind: I am OK you are OK, and takes the empathy-compromise-tolerance route, then the communication would be very effective.

USE OF DECENCY SKILLS IN EFFECTIVE COMMUNICATION

Type of Use	Sentence
(i) Least	I.
(ii) Frequently	Thank you.
(iii) Liberally	Will you please.
(iv) Reasonably	What is your opinion.
(v) Specifically	I am proud of you.
(vi) Particularly	I admit, I made a mistake.

We need to use certain DECENCY SKILLS to make the people interested in very beginning. Decency skills are the skills of civilized, well brought up, educated and self controlled people. These skills can be briefed under three heads—

Greeting Skills

Greeting skills are shown in using the customary ways of greeting people nicely saying 'Good Morning', 'Hellow', 'How are you' and 'Welcome' etc.

Examples

'Pleased to meet you'. 'Good day to you Sir'.
'Congratulations'. 'Thanks for this honour'.
Marvellous! Well done!
Beautiful! Wonderful!
Excellent! Really!

Politeness Skills

Politeness skills are an expression of one's sensitivity to the feelings and opinions of others; of one's respect for others; of one's gratitude to others. This discern what is appropriate to communicate using the expressions like 'excuse me', Please', 'Thank you', 'Very kind of you' etc.

Examples

Please excuse me.
I beg your pardon.

Never mind.
Please allow me to say.
I am sorry for being late.
Sorry to have disturbed you.
That is very kind of you.
Could you spare a few moments for me.
Will you please permit me to speak?
May I have your attention please.
Glad to meet you.
Please help yourself.
Please don't mistake me.

Kindness Skills

Kindness skills express one's good wishes for others and readiness to do some thing for others. KINDNESS IS LIKE A SUNSHINE ON A COLD DAY. KIND WORDS HEAL WOUNDED HEARTS. A Japani proverb says, "one kind word—Warms three Winters."

Examples

Thanks.	Thank you.	Thank God!
Please.	Please stop.	Please rest assured.
With great pleasure.	It is my pleasure.	What a pleasant surprise.
Sorry.	Excuse me.	Pardon.
You are welcome.	Welcome Sir.	Kindly.
May I help you?	By God's grace.	May God bless you.
It's all right.	It's fine.	Very good.
Allow me.	No mention.	Of course.
What an idea!		

Decency skills generate mutual trust and relationship by showing that one is not pre-occupied in his own things alone, but is genuinely interested in the other and can be constructive.

CORRECTIVE MEASURE

To communicate with people, first we have to look at our problem: "What I am saying, will the other person understand it in the same spirit; will he understand the words with the same meaning?" If we can concentrate on these aspects and change the way we are using our language, we can get a much better understanding. The second step is to look at the transmission, to avoid any noises, any distractions, any lack of interest. If so, we can see that environment of the training or the message is changed to facilitate communication. The third most difficult problem is obviously the problem of hostility. It does not come from outside, it comes from inside us as well as from the inside of the other person. This is where we have to look at our prejudices, our impulses and our life position. Are we approaching people: "I am OK- you are not OK" or "I am OK- you are OK"? Are we trying to understand their viewpoint? If this is the attitude we take, then communication will be successful.

CONCLUSION

A drop of ink can make millions think- that is the power of expression. Penned words or said words are not letters strung together but they are emotions and stimulators of emotions. A word can make or break relationship. Words are gift of god. Wrongly used, they embarrass and dishonour us. Be a positive creative communicator. Choose words, as carefully as an interior decorator selects each accessories.

PART II

PREFACE

Communication refers to the process to impart, convey or exchange the information, ideas or knowledge from one person to another by speech, writing or by other means who should understand it in the accurate sense.

Communication plays the most important role in every walk of life and in our every interaction with others. **Our effectiveness is highly correlated with our communication skills. This is key to success and our communication skill adds value, meaning and effectiveness in all our roles.**

Communication plays an important role at all times, especially during good time it builds pride and in tough time it maintains the spirit. **Communication is the life-blood of any organisation.** It determines how everything is managed, right from work processes to relationship in the organisation and its culture plus investors perception. **Effective communication skills are prerequisites to manage teams and groups, resolving interpersonal conflicts, handling negotiations and counselling employees etc. for the success of organisation.** Listening and responding, giving and receiving feedback are the important aspects of communication.

Communication is the process through which information is organised in meaningful ways to lead to desired actions. The ability to communicate meaningfully is becoming a key determinant to make effective decisions in the perspective of growth, innovation and sustainability for competitive advantage with the help of shared vision and collective efforts.

Communication is the act of transmitting an idea from one person to another. It involves—the communication — the message—the media —and the receiver. There is no communication, if no one is getting the message. Communication does not begin with the speaker but it begins with the receiver. Until and unless someone is getting the message, nothing is happening. Face-to-face meetings will bring clarity in communication.

HOW TO IMPROVE THE QUALITY OF CONVERSATION

When did you have a conversation at work that truly excited you? When you discovered new insights, heard counter--intuitive arguments to arrive at creative and novel solutions? **The conversation lies at the heart for talk to teach and inspire, review and provide feedback, plan and take decisions.** The conversation is essential to develop new ideas, share knowledge and experience, enhance individual and collective learning.

We are all aware of the importance of emotional conversations in our private lives—for building, trusting and intimate relationships within the family and friends. The display of emotions establish our authenticity and create the basis for appreciating one another. In the emerging knowledge based and service-intensive economy; work needs the same level of empathy, mutual understanding, trust and the emotional conversations which are the foundation for building such relationship.

HOW TO LISTEN BODY LANGUAGE AND WHAT IS THE REAL MESSAGE

A better listener use their ears and eyes and really tune in. Listening depends upon our willingness and ability. **Listeners understand the BODY LANGUAGE to arrive at WHAT IS THE REAL MESSAGE?**

The ways to improve our listening ability are as under:

(i) Take the listening responsibility of the communication process. Exclusively, the speaker is not responsible for communication. If necessary, stop them, ask the questions to make sure that the communication process is complete.

(ii) Identify the value moments in listening. Every once in a while somebody is writing some thing. Think what can I find that will be of value to me in terms of what is being said.

(iii) Take notes. The act of writing itself will help us to remember.

(iv) Imagine for a moment, that you had to make a report on what you are listening to. You probably would be taking notes and as such would be listening very carefully to record the contents in your report.

(v) When distractions occur in the listening process, stick with return to the contents.

(vi) Each one of us is provided with two ears and one mouth. Function of ears is to hear while of mouth to taste, eat and speak. We should use them in same proportion to identify the problem and use their cause and effect as an example.

As you know, there is another way and we can use our eyes to understand the body language of the speaker to arrive at what he is thinking and feeling. In order to determine face-to-face communication, the important factors are the words that were chosen and how those words were said, the verbal quality of things, the pauses, the tones and the inflection. The most important is to understand how the other person is thinking and how they are feeling. **Action speaks louder than words.** Perfect action and body language have always been one of the greatest assets of a communicator.

HOW TO EXPRESS WORDS TO MAKE A POSITIVE DIFFERENCE

Words do make a difference. They express our feelings and communicate messages. The mind is the gateway to the heart and the words you use are so enormously important. Thoughts provide us with words to express.

In persuading and motivating people to produce the desired results that are needed, the only tool is the written and spoken word. What managers do more than anything else is to communicate with—suppliers, customers, colleagues and above all with their own staff. Effective communication is fast becoming an area of core competence. Improve communication and you improve performance. The critical challenges faced in communicating effectiveness are in areas of: (i) Information, (ii) Channels, (iii) Feedback, (iv) Change, (v) Interdepartmental communication and (vi) Innovation which needs to be planned strategically including how to manage the relationship between data, information, knowledge and action for smooth running of organisation.

What difference do words make? Let me ask all of you a question. "How many of you have noticed that 90% of the troubles you anticipate, never take place?" Everybody said "That is right". I said in other words, "Out of the total bad things—we expect to happen, only about 10% really happen to us." You are what you are and where you are because of what is gone into your mind. Now you can change what you are and where you are by changing what goes into your mind. The expectancy does play a major role in our life.

For example, once upon a time, the all time best speaker said "As yu show, so shall yu reep", then computer people declared this input as 100% negative i.e. "Garbage In, Garbage Out". But when he corrected it to "As you sow, so you reap", they declared this input 100% positive. Thus if you put the (bad) negative stuff in; you get the negative stuff out. But when you put the good stuff in, you get the good stuff out. You see **what you put in your mind makes all the difference. The choice is yours. Every choice we make in life, literally has an end result.**

Why to pay the price for failure? Better we pay the price for success and enjoy its benefits. Optimism is absolutely the practical approach to life.

Just imagine, when a child is called stupid; what the picture is before him? If employer says that their personnel are lazy, does that inspire or encourage them to work harder? **Remember! that every choice has an end result. We need to understand that when we choose something, we literally are choosing the end results. Therefore, demonstrate the power of words; accordingly plan, prepare, use them expecting commitment and results.** It demonstrate the power of repetition. You see, the repetition is the mother of learning, father of action and that makes it the architect of accomplishment. Thus you can just do everything and anything for accomplishment and success. **You can do it and you were born to win.** However, failure is an event and you give it another shot to win. **Use the positive words, change your approach to life, change your attitude and keep busy so that some amazing things happen.** If you will buy these ideas and do above things, I am sure, you will be really at the top. **The right words, however few, could trigger many a brilliant ideas, bringing fresh life into your organisation.**

Just as a diamond is valued and recognised for its 4C's

(Colour, Carat, Cut and Clarity); similarly a organisation cherish values and achieve its goal by it's own 4 C's i.e. Competence, Commitment, Consistency and Communication. During verbal communication, maintain good positive tone which sounds cheerful, pleasant, courteous, helpful, interested, patient, sincere and moderate.

HOW TO COMMUNICATE BETTER AT WORK

Speaking is more powerful way of communicating than writing. The ability to speak well can boost your self-confidence and self-esteem. You can never succeed with people without mutual trust and understanding. Effective communication skill could just be the difference between success and you. **The tools of communication changes dynamically in technology, likes and dislikes, tastes and preferences.** In communication be polite and polished. Be audience friendly i.e. **'keep it short and simple' (KISS).** Don't forget the LAW i.e. Looks, Actions and Words. It is never too late to begin presenting the message in person by which you are in a stronger position to ensure that it is clearly understood, acknowledged and acted upon.

Employees often show concern about the quality and quantity of communication at work. Ineffective communication often results in poor cooperation and coordination, lower productivity, undercurrents of tension, gossip and rumours, increased turnover and absenteeism. Experience shows there are many ways to improve internal communication. Consider the following points while communicating better at work:

(i) Understand that communication is a two-way street. It involves giving information and getting feedback from employees. It is not finished when information is given.

(ii) Put more emphasis on face-to-face communication with employees. Don't rely mainly on bulletin boards, memos and other written communication.

(iii) Ask themselves, each time they give an instruction,

if the message is clear. Most vagueness is caused by failing to be specific. Example: Don't just tell an employee to "show more interest" in his or her work, but if an employee spends too much time chatting with others, be specific about it.

(iv) View information as "service to" employees and not "power over" them.

(v) Listen to employees; show respect for them when they speak. They will feel part of the team and will tend to be more dedicated and productive. One way: ask questions to show interest and clarify points.

(vi) Don't just talk open-door policy. Practice it by walking around and talking to employees. Allow people to disagree and to come up with new ideas.

(vii) Conduct one-on-one meetings. Ask each employee to coordinate with the manager and how the manager can help the employee to do a better job. Then share those things employees can do; to help the manager to do a better job.

(viii) Concentrate on building credibility with employees. Managers, who lack credibility and fail to create a climate of trust and openness aren't believed—no matter how hard they try to communicate.

Everyone needs to take responsibility for speaking and listening in a way that not only ensures clear communication but also makes it easier for others to understand and speak up.

CONCLUSION

Your decent expression opens up a whole new world of opportunities to enable you to win over thousands of hearts inspite of the difference in ideology. As said by CONFUCIUS (Legendary Chinese Philosopher) in order to understand—we need to experience: ***"I hear and I forget. I see and I remember. I experience and I understand."***

PART III

TIPS FOR EFFECTIVE COMMUNICATION— A PROCESS OF CLOSENESS

For effective communication to take place, it must be OK to tell the truth, the whole truth and to clarify feelings. This means sharing good things as well as things felt to be negative.

Good communication depends first on a healthy and trusty relationship. When people are reluctant to share the truth, they don't have great confidence in their own ability to handle the response or they feel that risk involved is too great. But, by not telling the truth, you build a barrier-you have no connection with the others, and thus no closeness. Honesty brings people closer, because it removes barriers.

COMMUNICATION IN A GROUP SETTING

In order to make sure that your ideas and feelings are effectively communicated in a group, we must take care of the following points:

1. Clearly 'own' your messages by using personal pronouns such as I and my, rather than 'most people', 'our group'. Seek to clarify your ideas before communication.
2. Examine the true purpose of each communication.
3. Make your message complete and specific, for making your intentions and assumptions clear.
4. Consult with others, where appropriate, in planning the communications.
5. Make your verbal and nonverbal messages consistent with each other. Be mindful, while you communicate of the overtones as well as the basic content of your message.
6. Repeat your message in different ways, if necessary.
7. Ask for feedback concerning the way your messages are being received.

8. Make the message appropriate to the listener-remember to whom you are talking to and their level of understanding etc.
9. Draw out, Probe fully for each explanation—or stop talking to allow the other person to complete the expression of his thoughts more fully.
10. Don't interrupt.
11. Check out what you've heard.
12. Present one idea at a time and get acceptance of each before moving on to the next.
13 Be explicit—say what you mean as precisely as possible.
14. Describe your feelings by name, action, or figure of speech to make yourself more clear and understandable.
15. Describe other members' behaviour without evaluating or interpreting it. Take the opportunity, when it arises, to convey something of help or value of the receiver.
16. Follow up your communication.
17. Communicate for tomorrow as well as today.
18. Be sure your actions support your communication. Be a good listener.
19. Share your ideas and feelings—set a trusting example.

COMMUNICATION OVER TELEPHONE

In view of exorbitant rise in the telephone rates, it is absolutely essential that use of telephone conversation on STD is resorted to only in dire necessity. We have E-Mail Facility and Fax Machines with us and it will be economical to send a long message preferably on E-Mail or alternatively on Fax than conveying it on STD.

A few points are summed up below which can be kept in mind while using telephone for STD calls or otherwise.

1. Keep index of frequently used numbers to save time.
2. Depending upon necessity, send requisition forms to Telephone Operator to book the trunk calls or STD.

3. Talking on STD should he preferably done when the person concerned is directly available on the number called since calling a person through the board consumes time. Whenever a person has to be called through the board, it is better and cheaper to book a P.P. Call.
4. Acknowledge caller promptly by speaking your name and knowing his name.
5. Connect the caller quickly.
6. Before attending a call which has been booked, keep a pen and message pad on your table with a list of points to be talked by you and your colleagues, in order to avoid unnecessary loss of time in searching for the relevant papers after the call is matured.
7. Jotting down messages as they are given and if essential, reading messages back to caller as a check.
8. We should cultivate the habit of speaking messages to the point, clearly and quickly in a very pleasant voice.
9. Be precise and brief in talk since calls are charged for time as well as distance.
10. After booking the call, if you are leaving your office, please inform the operator as to where you will be available or advise the operator to try later, on your return.
11. If after booking the call you have talked to the person concerned through any other phone directly or call has come from other side, please inform the operator immediately so that we do not waste money by calling the same person again.

9

Team Management— The Art of Collectiveness

PREAMBLE

I think the word "TEAM" probably stands for "TOGETHER EVERYONE ACCOMPLISHES MORE". An organisation cannot function successfully by one man alone. It can only be run efficiently by a team of men acting together. Building a good, strong team is, therefore, the first step towards success.

An organisation is the collection of employees. The success of an organisation depends on the ability of such efficient and effective small teams of employees, within it, **to work together to attain the common goals and objectives of the total organisation.** The members of the team must be committed to achieve the goals by involving all team members.

Working together of people for collective responsibility increases a strong team spirit by coming together of their hearts, minds, values, vision and culture. Therefore, coming together is beginning, keeping together is progress and working together is success. The spirit of sustaining excellence is a trend to achieve success by team work—to maximise the creativity, intellect, decision making and problem solving contribution of entire human resource by their vision, values and initiativeness. You have to delegate responsibility to your team. Increased responsibility leads to people becoming more involved in their jobs. People work for satisfaction, challenge and recognition. The individual needs to develop his capabilities to build, lead, inspire and energise his team; so that he can enhance effectiveness to achieve overall organisational goals. In order to build successful teams around him; the each member must consist speed, simplicity, integrity and self confidence to continuously grow and prosper.

TEAM WORK AND TEAM SPIRIT

TEAM WORK is the ability to work together towards a common vision. TEAM SPIRIT is the ability to direct individual achievement towards organisational objectives. By working together, ordinary people can perform extraordinary excellence. The groups are formed where members interact primarily to share information and to make decisions to help each member perform within the specified area of responsibility. But teams generate positive synergy through coordinated efforts. A team must have few special characteristics to ensure increase in performance, productivity and satisfaction.

WHY TEAM MANAGEMENT

(i) Obtain constructive guidance on group objectives through a wide variety of sources.

(ii) Keep pace with the latest developments relating to work teams.

(iii) Examine a host of issues including changes in performance measurement, the information system, rewards and compensation etc. through a broad-based outlook.

(iv) Gain advice on the best ways to overcome common pitfalls.

HOW TO ENCOURAGE TEAM WORK ON YOUR EMPLOYEES

Use the following tactics to cut down on rivalry and encourage collaboration among your employees:

(i) Publicize the group goals. Prepare a simple mission statement for your employees. Outline common goals and explain why they are important.

(ii) Define roles. Avoid unnecessary rivalries by clearly identifying each individuals role within the group.

(iii) In order to empower a work-force; you need to listen, enhance self-esteem, provide constructive feedback, encourage innovation etc. Give your team the power to make decisions and hold them accountable.

(iv) Give people a sense of ownership in what they are doing as a group.

(v) Share information. Talk directly to the group.

(vi) Reinforce the team concept. When your staff has done well, praise the entire effort without singling out individuals.

WHY DO TEAMS FAIL TO DELIVER

The team can fail to deliver the desired results due to the following reasons:

(i) Unclear or vague goals.

(ii) Lack of clarity or purpose.

(iii) Lack of Management support and low priority to team building.

(iv) Ineffective team leadership.

These failures can be avoided with proper advance planning.

HOW TO DEVELOP TEAM WORK

It is essential for the team to appraise the strengths and weaknesses constantly. The successful teams will have a combination of the qualities summed up on the "TEAM WORK" which are detailed below:

T—TRUST: High performance teams are characterised by high mutual trust among members. This feeling of trust depends upon truthfulness, transparency and the readiness to fulfil promises and assurances. But caution is also there that **"Trust is fragile. It takes a long time to build but can be easily destroyed and is hard to regain"**. Trust needs to be earned and it cannot be demanded.

E—ENTHUSIASM: Without enthusiasm nothing great was ever achieved. Enthusiasm is also the greatest motivator known to man. We develop enthusiasm by developing feeling of self-efficacy and self-esteem.

A—AMBITION TO SUCCEED: The burning inner drive to achieve the predetermined goals must be there in each of the team member.

M—MUTUAL INTEREST: Every team player must aspire for a common purpose. But how can it be possible with every member having difference in opinion, personality, attitude, expectations and aspirations? Of course, it is possible if members sacrifice some of their personal interest and reach to a point where mutuality of interests of individual goals and organisation common goals can be achieved.

W—WORKABILITY OF GOALS: The goals determined by the team must be realistic and capable of being worked. It is far better idea to talk in more moderate terms about goals.

O—OPENNESS: Willingness to share ideas and information freely should prevail in a team which brings new ideas, approaches, skills and talent to the organisation and satisfaction to the team people.

R—RESILIENCE: The team members should have the ability to bounce back from disappointment and recover strength quickly. Thomas Edison suffered hundreds of failures before he finally invented the light bulb. Try and try again must be the guiding principle behind every action.

K—KEY RESULT AREAS: KRAs are the statements of the most important results expected from a team player holding specific job. KRAs are important because they provide goals, put the emphasis on outputs and not on inputs. Also, they provide a basis for appraisals and performance management.

PRE-REQUISITES FOR A SUCCESSFUL TEAM

The followings are the pre-requisites for a successful team:

(i) Formulate team objectives carefully.
(ii) Break long-term objectives into short-term plan.
(iii) Allocate a clear deadline for each plan.
(iv) Decide what style of team is suitable.
(v) Choose the leader on merit.
(vi) Evaluate and select candidates on merit.
(vii) Try to establish strong bonds among team members.
(viii) Encourage contributions from every team member.
(ix) Give your team the freedom to arrive at its own decisions.
(x) Find some easy way of displaying team progress.
(xi) When trouble brews in any team relationship, resolve it quickly.
(xii) Look for ways to use conflict constructively.
(xiii) Use impartial fact-finding as a method for defusing conflict.
(xiv) Meet informally or formally to discuss team progress.
(xv) Give agendas in advance of the meeting, to give teams the time to prepare.
(xvi) Encourage free-flow of communication between team members.
(xvii) Arrange contacts with other teams within an organisation.
(xviii) Tell individuals they are doing a good job to build team morale.
(xix) Build a plan but be prepared to change it even at the most fundamental level.
(xx) Chalk out a result plan.
(xxi) Devise a reliable yardstick to measure team progress.
(xxii) Identify and analyse performance problems.

WHO IS RESPONSIBLE FOR TEAM BUILDING

Now comes the most important and crucial question. The unanimous one word answer to this critical question is **'The Leader'**. An old saying *goes* **"A good teacher teaches, a better teacher explains and the best teacher inspires"**. The same is true for the leader of a team who must have to be transformational leader with burning spirit and also can transform an individual into a team player.

Communication gap is quite often the root cause of strained relationships in an organisation and posses a serious threat to the existence of the congenial atmosphere. It is the art of decently expressing free and frank exchange of views, with no reservation in putting forth altogether the suggestions to be cultivated. Again, a transformational leader is needed to provide vision and sense of mission, instills pride, gains respect and trust. He communicates high expectations and expresses important purposes in simple ways. This type of the leader inspires followers to transcend their own self interest and put aside petty differences for the good of the organisation.

Leader need to listen, enhance self-esteem, provide constructive feedback, encourage innovation etc. We must be able to give power to the team, to make decisions and hold them accountable.

QUALITIES OF TEAM MANAGEMENT LINKER

The Team Management Linker often brings in a fresh way of looking at things. The identified linking skills that encompass internal linking, external linking and informal linking are as follows:

(i) Listen before deciding.
(ii) Keep team members upto date on a regular basis.
(iii) Available and responsive to people's problems.
(iv) Develop a balanced team.
(v) Allocate work to people based on their capabilities.
(vi) Encourage respect, understanding and trust amongst

team members.

(vii) Delegate work, which it is not essential for them to do.

(viii) Set an example and agree high quality standards with the team.

(ix) Set achievable targets for the team, but always press them for improved performance.

(x) Coordinate and represent team members.

(xi) Involve team members in the problem solving of key issues.

The Team Management Linker understands other people's view. He knows when to talk and when to listen. He picks up the key points and work on the problems raised and report back. He allows opportunities for people to put their views before decisions.

PRINCIPLES OF TEAM-BRIEFING MEETINGS

Team-briefing meetings have the following basic principles to ensure that the team is working to its maximum potential:

(i) Face-to-face contact is important.

(ii) The meetings should be kept small.

(iii) They should be led by the team leader but not necessarily chaired by him or her.

(iv) The meetings should be regular.

(v) The issues should be relevant to the tasks and should concern everyone.

(vi) Information flow must be 'two-way'.

The regular meetings should be conducted to understand each other's work. The importance of meetings is to get work done in an atmosphere, where people could keep upto date with views of each others. The compliment for achievement has to be specific and sincere to encourage members. We must also take time to show appreciation for other members of the team. A sense of appreciation for each other should be maintained because it took everyone working together to solve the specific problem.

TEAM ASSESSMENT

In team assessment, we need to review the followings:

(i) Are we making optimum use of available resources?
(ii) Is our team operating at peak efficiency?
(iii) Are our decisions the best ones?
(iv) Could other teams perform better than us? If so, why?
(v) Where do we under perform?
(vi) What obstacles team needs to overcome?

CONCLUSION

A winning team turns conflict into cooperation by focusing on common goals and develop an environment where people feel comfortable to speak and contribute their ideas to achieve the goals. Now it is quite evident that when the team culture is cultivated in any organisation, people derive strength from each other through the **JOY OF WORKING TOGETHER.** Team members develop a high level of affinity among themselves and become aware of each others' needs and potential contributions. Ultimately, strong feeling of togetherness and openness develop among themselves. A strong 'we' feeling and 'we' orientation among team members created serves many purposes. It gives stamina for people to meet turbulent times and enhances problem solving capabilities for the team, benefiting the organisation at large.

10

Time Management— Exactness in Work

PART I

Time is a unique invisible resource because it has an end. **Time is the only resource that must be used as early as it is desired.** It must be used at a fixed rate of 60 seconds per minute and 60 minutes per hour since you can't get more. We can control, how we use our time. **We have no choice whether to spend it or not but only how to use the time. Once we have wasted time, its gone and it cannot be saved.** If, you take care of the minutes, the hours will take care of themselves. Effective time management is the key to the growth.

Have you ever said yourself "I did not have enough time". You are not alone, since **you have exactly the same number of hours per day, equal to ALL SUCCESSFUL PEOPLE.** Then **"How is it that you are not the one, out of all successful people?" It depends upon you -- "How best results, you can achieve in relation to use of your time?"** You invest your time to concentrate and ensure your maximum efforts on the **IMPORTANT AND HIGH RETURN TASKS.**

The 24 hours each day are yours to invest wisely or spend foolishly. How you manage your time will spell the difference between success and failure, profit and loss, satisfaction and dissatisfaction. Use your time efficiently and wisely. Here are few tips on how to achieve time mastery.

IMPORTANT ASPECTS OF TIME

(i) **Time** is a valuable resource of your's as well as that of our every employee. Unless you learn to manage it well, you cannot manage anything well. A **fraction of time cannot be bought by a ton of Gold.** You can decide how to spend time. Time is man's most precious commodity and **have optimum utilisation of every fraction of second.**

(ii) **Time** should never be spend; it should be invested. When time is wasted, i.e. used to no purpose, it is spent, not invested. It pays no interest and no dividend.

(iii) **Time** invested in work and employment should be aimed at improving productivity — accomplishing more in few hours.

(iv) **Time** invested in "Utilities"—sleeping, eating, personal care—should be aimed at strengthening your personal support system.

(v) **Time discretionary should be invested in:**

- Building friendships and cementing family ties;
- Maintaining your health;
- Improving your skills and knowledge and contributing to the good of your home and your community; and
- Relaxing in ways that refresh your body, mind and spirit.

(vi) Use intelligence before you transcript the time:
For a perfect instance, I quote the story about the old shopkeeper on Main Street who placed a grandfather clock in the front window of his store. Over the years the shopkeeper noticed that a distinguished-looking man would walk by the store every day at noon . . . pause in front of the grandfather clock . . . pull out a

pocket watch . . . and carefully set the time.

One day, when the gentleman paused in front of grandfather clock, the shopkeeper asked the man why he set his watch every day. The man replied, *"I'm the foreman at the town mill,"* he said. *"I blow the quitting whistle at 5:00 each day, and I want to be sure it goes off exactly on time."*

The old shopkeeper gave him a startled look—and then burst out laughing. The man stepped back and asked indignantly, *"What's so funny?" "I'm sorry,"* replied the shopkeeper, *"I didn't mean to be rude. But I just had to laugh. You see, all these years I've been setting my grandfather clock to your 5:00 whistle?"*

CUT WASTED TIME

Attack the problem of wasted time with the following steps:

(i) Identify sources of wasted time. Then answer these questions:

(a) What causes you to lose valuable time?
(b) What is the scope of this problem?
(c) How much productive time is lost by it?
(d) How deeply does it cut into your leisure time?

(ii) Plan specific actions to reduce wasted time. Divide the problem into the time you waste and the time others waste. Begin by setting goals, in terms of causes to eliminate and time to be saved. Then specify how you will accomplish these goals by changing your habits and exercising discipline over your behaviour. For others under your authority or influence, develop a program of organization, training, motivation and time control. Commit your goals to writing.

(iii) Implement actions. This will require initiative and persistence. No matter how strongly motivated you may be, others will need much persuasion. Maintain a chart of the weekly and monthly progress you make toward your goals.

EVALUATE WORTH OF YOUR TIME

Based upon 8 hours per day and 300 working days per year the following chart display the true worth of your time:

Annual Salary Rs.	*Worth of One Hour a Day Annually Rs.*	*Worth of Every Hour Rs.*
1,00,000	12,500	41.67
1,50,000	18,750	62.50
2,00,000	25,000	83.33
2,50,000	31,250	104.17
3,00,000	37,500	125.00
3,50,000	43,750	145.83
4,00,000	50,000	166.67
4,50,000	56,250	187.50
5,00,000	62,500	208.33
5,50,000	68,750	229.17
6,00,000	75,000	250.00

The above chart makes it explicitly clear that when you waste time, you are also wasting money. Therefore, identify your biggest time wasters and their causes, to find their long lasting solutions.

CONTROL TIME

You can control time by the following steps:

(i) **Establish a time frame for the activity you wish to keep under control.** Fix your goals in your mind and enter them on a calendar or appointment book. If your activity is part of a larger organisational plan, the deadline may also be displayed.

(ii) **Measure progress towards the goal.** Keep track of

your time, check your appointment calendar, or examine a control chart.

(iii) **Take steps to keep progress moving.** Change your approach to speed up progress. Add resources, use faster equipment, or delegate work to a subordinate.

TECHNIQUES TO ALERT YOU TO TIME TRAPS

(i) **Control the Telephone.** Set aside one period during the day to make and receive calls. Give priority to what you are doing, not to a ringing telephone.

(ii) **Limit social visits.** Don't make extended conversations comfortable for the other person. Say you are busy at the moment, or offer to schedule an appointment. Limit physical access to casual visitors.

(iii) **Expect idle time to crop up when you least expect it.** Keep a block of productive activities in reserve for such opportunities.

(iv) **Increase delegation.** Assign routine work and their decisions to subordinates.

(v) **Check time estimates.** Periodically assess how realistic your estimates are. Adjust your time budget accordingly.

(vi) **Don't over commit your time.** There will always be new and unexpected demands placed upon you.

(vii) **Understand that every completion deadline invokes a related starting deadline.** Proceed to the next activity without delay.

(viii) **Decide quickly on small matters.** There are many small matters to deal with and an occasional misfire won't cause much damage.

For an illustration, I quote a story of Akbar and Birbal. Badshah Akbar asked his Navratnas, "How many crows are their in all in Agra? It is important, that we have this information immediately. You have to give me the correct answer, or else there will be serious trouble, I warn you." The Navratanas were scarred of punishment since no body knew the number of crows in Agra city. Birbal was silent but after some time he said, "Your Majesty, there are exactly ten thousand six hundred and sixty-six crows in all the Agra city." Badshah Akbar asked "Are you sure, Birbal? We shall have the crows counted to make sure the number you have said is correct." Birbal said calmly, "By all means. Your majesty, but I cannot be sure that all the crows will remain in Agra till the counting is completed. Many relatives and friends of these crows may come to visit them in Agra and so it will increase the number. Many crows may go from Agra and visit their friends and relations in Delhi and so there will be less than number I give you. I can surely say that at this moment there are ten thousand six hundred and sixty six crows in all in Agra city." The Badshah burst out laughing and said, "Birbal, you are amazing!" Birbal used the concept of approximation by his knowledge, common sense, intelligence and wisdom to complete the work in less time.

(ix) **Form the completion habit.** Whenever possible, finish one task before starting another.

A specimen chart showing "THE BIGGEST TIME WASTERS, THEIR CAUSES AND SOLUTIONS" is enclosed.

MASTER TIME

The few keys to time mastery are:

(i) **Find out where your time goes**. You can do this by:
- Make an activities time analysis. Make a list of all your tasks, whether recurring or unique, and decide how much time to devote to each and when.
- Keep a daily log of your activities.

(ii) **Learn where your time goes**. Treat time as your personal capital and invest it in activities that can pay off handsomely.

(iii) **Minimize your time commitments**. Don't take on more work than you can comfortably handle. Limit your activities to those that fit in with the goals.

(iv) **Sort out what needs to be done now and what can wait**. Use ABC analysis. It is wiser to devote your efforts to the 20% of problems that account for 80% of your difficulties. Then determine whether these problems are:

- Class A: The most troublesome and time-consuming, but the most rewarding when solved.
- Class B: Those that fall between the most and least rewarding.
- Class C: The least troublesome and time-consuming, but the least rewarding when solved.

(v) **Cut down on time-wasting activities**. It's a fact of life that we waste more time in little important pursuits than we invest in more productive activities.

(vi) **Be ruthless about distractions**. Be ruthless with situations and people who intrude upon your personal time.

(vii) **Locate information in a hurry**. Searching for and handling information consumes upto 20% of your time for which you need to evolve system.

(viii) **Build a time control plan that fits your job and personality**. Based upon a knowledge of how time influences your life, you can prepare a daily agenda. Maintain an appointment calendar, planning chart, citing what, where, when, how and who; your schedule will involve.

(ix) **Break the defer action habit**. The causes of defer action include fear of failure or waiting for the right time.

(x) **Use other people's time to your advantage**. Persuade others to help you willingly, to get your work done. Delegate tasks they are capable of carrying out.

(xi) **Be creative with your time**. Your time may be consumed by tasks and procedures that are no longer efficient. Discard costly habits and replace them with more time effective methods.

(xii) **Add hours to your time by working smarter, not harder**. Modern technology—electronic mail, the fax machine, etc. accomplish more in less time.

(xiii) **Identify and stop work that makes no sense**. The work that does not contribute to improve productivity, quality, value, customer satisfaction, employees benefit and profit; to be identified and should be stopped.

You can determine by time management which of the things are important and how effectively we can use time to produce the best results. Simultaneously, we can control the biggest time wasters by identifying their causes and solutions. You can also plan to manage your time better by help of 'Day Planners', 'Things to do today' or by delegating more work etc. However, it is important that you define your goals, objectives and action plan in specific terms and establish a realistic and achievable time frame for their accomplishment. The time management says not more time but a stress free better life.

SUMMARY OF THE BIGGEST TIME WASTERS, THEIR CAUSES AND SOLUTIONS

Time Wasters	*Causes*	*Solutions*
1. Attempting Too Much	• Over ambitious and inordinate need to achieve. • Over response. • Over desire to appear cooperative.	• Ask yourself what you are trying to prove. Be realistic. Keep perspective. Stop killing yourself. • Limit your response to the real demands of the situation. • Stay Uninvolved, if others can handle it. Stop saying yes, just because you want to be appreciated.
2. Confused Responsibility or Authority	• Failure to clarify precise responsibilities. • Job overlap. • Responsibility without authority.	• Prepare list of responsibilities for approval. • Identify and eliminate areas of duplication. • Insist on commensurate authority coupled equal to responsibility.
3. Drop-in Visitor	• No plans for unavailability. • Expecting subordinates to check with you excessively. • Inability to terminate visits.	• Recognize that "open door" does not mean physically open, but open to those who need assistance. Implement quiet hour; screening; hideaway. • Manage by exception. • Meet others outside your office. Stand up upon entry and keep standing.
4. Inability to Say No	• Possess capabilities in demand. • Not knowing how to refuse. • Can't say no to boss.	• Concentrate your efforts. • Count to ten before saying yes. When saying no, give reasons, suggest alternatives. • Say no by showing list of agreed-upon priorities. If boss insists, acquiesce, but advise what you fear will not get done.

5. Inadequate Controls and Progress Reports	• Unaware of importance. • Lack enforcement of controls.	• Recognize that controls which monitor progress and correct variance, thus guaranteeing satisfactory performance. • Recognize this means, you might as well not have controls.
6. Inadequate Planning.	• Unaware of importance. • Assumption that "it is futile to plan. • Have plan in mind but believe it is not important enough to write it down.	• Recognize that every hour in effective planning saves four in execution and gets better results. Recognize that most managers tend to waste time in the same way everyday. • Recognize that no memory is infallible, and that no to do list is complete until priorities and deadlines are met.
7. Inadequate Staff	• Lack training. • Limited finances.	• Recognize that without competent staff, effective delegation is impossible. Make staff training a priority. • Conduct cost benefit analysis. Demonstrate what additional staff would do at what cost.
8. Incomplete Information	• Lack of System. • Lack of authority to require information needed. • Indecision or delay by others in providing needed information.	• Determine what information is needed. Then ensure its availability, reliability and timeliness. • Clarify authority. Use response deadlines. Take problem to boss, if unsuccessful. • "Unless I hear", Meet boss to explain importance of information.
9. Ineffective Delegation	• Can do the job better and faster. • Overcontrol. • More comfortable "doing" than "managing."	• Lower standards to what is acceptable, not your own level of performance. Avoid perfectionism. • Relax. Emphasize goal-accomplishment, not methods. Measure results, not activities. • Remember the job of the manager is managing, not doing.

Time Wasters	Causes	Solutions
10. Lack of Self-discipline	• Lack objectives or standards. • Not following up. • Leaving tasks unfinished.	• Set objectives in Key result areas. Develop standards (conditions that will exist when the job is done well). • Recognize that **people do what you inspect—not what you expect**—and the same goes for you. • Complete tasks before putting them down. Handle it once. Get it done the first time.
11. Leaving Tasks Unfinished	• Lack objective, priorities, deadlines. • Responding to the urgent. • Cluttered desk/personal disorganization.	• Set objectives and arrange in order of importance. Set deadlines on all important tasks. • Recognize that urgent matters rarely are as important as they seem. • Resist tendency to overreact, thus interrupting other tasks. • Get organized to permit effective control of tasks. Be systematic in handling information.
12. Management by Crisis	• Failure to anticipate problems. • Overreaction (treating problems as crises). • Fire fighting. • Lack of purpose. • Too many/too few meetings.	• Expect the unexpected. Ask where can go wrong. List potential problems and develop steps to prevent them, if possible. • Limit you response by : (a) ignoring problems which can be ignored (b) delegating others (c) handling only those which you alone can take care of. • Recognize that it is more important to prevent new fires from developing than to put out old ones. • Don't meet without a purpose or agenda. Only those needed should attend. Allow for appropriate planning. • Test need for regular meetings. Occasionally don't hold one; see what happens. Or cut time in half for those tending to last a long time.

13. Meetings.	• Failure to summarise conclusions and follow up.	• Summarize conclusions to ensure agreement and remind participants about assignments. Ensure effective follow-up.
14. Paperwork	• Indecision. • Over filing. • Lack system.	• Read it once, and handle it. Do it now; 80% of daily intake can be disposed of on first handling. Don't hoard it. • Answer on original when copy not essential. Or use back of original for copy of your response. • Reduce copies, standardize forms; file selectively and alphabetically, and with cross references; control record retention.
15. Personal Disorganization	• Ego (viewed by some as a symbol of busyness, importance, indispensability). • Fear loss of control. • Fear of forgetting.	• Recognize excessive paper may also symbolize indecision, procrastination, insecurity, confusion of priorities. • Use project plan sheets to provide better control than keeping all files on cluttered desk. • Proper calendaring and use of contact logs is excellent memory substitute. No need to remember what can be retrieved.
16. Poor Communication	• Use of wrong channel. • Differing value systems. • Lack of feedback.	• Select appropriate channel (phone, letter, memo, conference). • Recognize that experience and environment create different backgrounds for interpreting communication. • Get feedback to ensure understanding. Take corrective action.
17. Procrastination	• Thinking "I work best under pressure". • Ego trip (crisis creating).	• Recognize this assumption as pure rationalization. • It is dangerous to recognize tendency to allow a crisis to develop, so you can assume the role of "hero" in solving it.

Time Wasters	*Causes*	*Solutions*
	• Habit of doing the easy or trivial first, postponing the difficult.	• Great danger here—that which may not get done is the most vital. Get it done first.
18. Socializing	• Need to change pace and desire for change in scenery. • Desire to stay informed. • Thinking it is important for your business.	• Control the urge, and when indulging it, be thoughtful of others. Don't interrupt them. Take breaks where no one is working. • Plan to obtain necessary information on systematic basis. • Distinguish between keeping lines of communication open and needless socializing.
19. Telephone Interruptions	• No plan for handling. • Inability to terminate conversation. • Lack of delegation.	• Develop plan to screen, delegate, consolidate. Set hours for taking calls. • Preset time limit ("Yes, I can talk for a few minutes") • Delegate more. Refer calls to delegates. Plan calls. List points to be discussed.
20. Travel	• Purpose unclear. • Poor use of time en-route. • Stacked desk upon return.	• Clarify purpose, objectives. Explore alternatives to travel, such as bringing other person to you, telephone, conference call, letter. • Keep folder for Reading, Writing. Discussion. Keep lists for Thinking, Planning, Dictation. • Devise plan with staff to handle work in your absence. Assistant could send list or copies of correspondence.

PART II

WHAT IS TIME MANAGEMENT

Time management is nothing but self management. Time management is a personal process, which requires a lot of commitment, patience willingness and efforts from oneself. The idea is to use time optimally.

We need to decide what is important, what is critical, what is to be done first and what follows thereafter. Discriminate the work and divide into categories like urgent, important, ordinary. With this, we may be able to get 75% results by just doing 20% work on the **important and high return task.** List out detail of your objectives. **Why, what, when, who, where is to be completed and how? First work faster on the important, urgent ones and high return tasks.** Divide rest of the tasks as (i) not urgent but important, (ii) urgent but not important, (iii) not urgent and not important to include in your execution schedule. **Control only the things that really matters instead of controlling everything.** Once goals are chalked-out, there could be plenty of tasks on-hand and thus the importance of time management becomes all the more significant. **Work smarter but not harder.** Sitting for long hours with no positive end results does not mean that the time was being used effectively. **Killing time is committing suicide on instalment basis. If the time management techniques could be adopted, the rewards could certainly be significant.**

HOW TO OBTAIN THE BEST OUT OF YOUR TIME

The question arises whether you and your organisation spending and investing your time wisely? **Time is precious.** Time is intangible, invisible and inaudible. Time waits for no one. **Time once lost is gone forever.** No replacement. No reversal. Investing your time and energy is like investing your money. Success is directly related to how we spend our time. **The most successful are the ones that make the best use of their time.**

Time is of much greater value to us than almost all of our material possessions. You need to decide, how to spend your precious time. It is our personal choice as to how we spend our time wisely. **A little advance planning everyday could result in the most productive use of our time. How you spend your time is more important than how you spend your money.** Therefore, evaluate the tasks before you and decide which one will pay-off in the end and establish their priorities. Pick the task that will help you to build new skills or insights. Use better tools and techniques to understand insights. Some opportunities comes only once in a life-time and grab such chances. Reshuffle your schedule or delegate work to make it happen. Delegate tasks that subordinates could handle. Thus, time is most important resource of you and your organisation which should be utilised effectively.

HOW TO HANDLE TIME MANAGEMENT

Time management is basically focussed on self-discipline. You can have a 'quick ones' card which speak about those tasks, which could take a few minutes like making a call, sending a reminder, signing a few documents that are pending and so on. Effective time management can always save you a little more time to avoid you from last moment tension, thus enhancing your creativity. **You may be doing your best but imagine a situation, when you will be even more productive because you can manage your time even better. A little self-discipline can do wonders to your output.**

There are variety of approaches available as to what should be the sequence to carry-out the task. One should go through the various suggestions and then finally adopt as to what suits the best. A highly methodical approach can be useful to tackle the highly ambiguous and complex jobs. Time is life. To waste one's time is wasting one's life. You can manage your time by taking care of followings:

(i) Make it a habit to list all your tasks and activities for the day.

(ii) Draw up a weekly time schedule detailing all the regular and essential activities.

(iii) Decide your priorities at a time.

(iv) Review your time-table to determine if some areas are getting an unfair share of your time.

(v) Allow uninterrupted time to work on high priority tasks by delegating duties to junior staff.

(vi) Keep some flexible, unallocated time available for dealing with unforeseen problems.

(vii) Make sure your records cover everything important and keep them up-to-date.

(viii) Work out a reminder system by writing dates or appointments on a calendar or in a diary for each task.

HOW TO HANDLE TIME-MANAGEMENT WITH HUMAN RESOURCE

Human Resource Management provides to business, a cutting edge since they **drive the knowledge business.** The successful organisation use their wisdom to build a culture of excellence like.....

(i) They spend more time selecting right employees than on training and developing. They delay filling a position until they are sure that they have identified the individual with the right talents for the job.

(ii) They spend more time with the best performers to yield the greatest return than with the weak performers. **A top performer will produce more with greater success in less time and is likely to out perform all others.** Invest time in talented people.

(iii) If an employee often fails to complete job on time, assign him an earlier deadline to built in a time cushion than you normally give to others.

(iv) They spend more time rewarding, recognising, reinforcing and celebrating employees for doing things right and to out-perform the standards set by their best employees. Thus maximise your most precious resource.

The modern mind is ruled by technological advancement and you still depend on human emotions. Unless you attach emotions with features of the job, you can't ensure the success. Do not think that you can make a better decision since you are taking more time to think. **It is basically your intelligent approach that would help in making better decision.** Develop a habit and sense of judgement regarding identification of jobs that are to be done. Delegate job to the right person, who has good intensions to complete the job in time. **In fact, time is a unique resource and there is always a scope for continuous improvement. The passion plays an important role for creating difference in building excellent organisation to achieve consistently consistent performance.**

IS TIME—TRUE WEALTH

The real wealth is having enough money with enough time—to do whatever you like and whenever you want. Time is money and we have to take full advantage of the available time.

Time is our far more precious commodity than gold — because once it is gone, it is gone forever. If you lose your job, you can always get another job. If you lose money in a bad investment, you can always try to make more money. But you can never get back the time, you have misused or lost. Many highly professionals have the enough money to buy and do what they want but most of them do not have the time. They have to keep working at their jobs, day in and day out to maintain their life-styles. **Therefore, spend your time wisely.**

The difficult tasks can be performed even in a less time and effort by wisely using certain levers. Lever means "to make lighter" which is an fittest description of the power of leverage. How corporation use leverage? **Hiring employees** is the most easy way, business owners leverage their time.

For example Henry Ford built a Model of Car by himself and he could have pocketed the entire benefit. But by working sole, he was able only to built a car or two each year. Ford was smart enough to leverage his time and talents by teaching his employees and built thousands of car each year and become one of the richest men in history. That is what the expression **"working smarter, not harder"** is all about.

The secret to building a fortune is compounding which is the time-honoured way to wealth creation. The ultimate tool for leveraging time and money is exponential growth, which enable your money to grow in multiples instead of growing step by step. In linear equation, your money grows step-by-step, whereas in exponential growth your money grows in multiplication known as **"Squaring"**. Some other examples for compounding are Franchising and Network Marketing

IT'S YOUR TURN-NEVER TO MISS THE OPPORTUNITY

In order to succeed, you don't have to possess "Star" talent like Amitabh Bachchan or Sachin Tendulkar. You don't have to be a born genius like Albert Einstein or Bill Gates. **Even the ordinary people can deliver extraordinary results by using their vision, courage and perseverance. You can do it—you have all the skills needed to succeed in it.**

The best is yet to come! It's your turn! to ensure that opportunities are never missed. Otherwise, someone else just take advantage of them first! Therefore, always remember that **you have to seize the opportunities as and when they are presented to you;** not when you think that you are ready for them. **Don't wait any longer!** Don't defer till tomorrow, what you can do today.

11

Creativity and Innovation—Scientific Logics

PART I

CREATIVITY IS THE THINKING OF NEW IDEAS, WHILE INNOVATION IS MAKING THEM HAPPEN. Without new ideas, there cannot be innovation. Creativity in the organization brings in the uniqueness and freshness into one's work. If you wish to achieve creativity, the knowledge is pre-requisite:

जीवन क्या है मौसम की खिड़की पर,
सपनों की चमकीली सी चिलमन है।
परदा गिर जाये तो निशी हर निशी है,
परदा उठ जाये तो दिन ही दिन है।।

CREATIVITY

Introduction

The introduction of new products are challenges of life and death for many companies. The improvement of existing products and the introduction of new products become an essential on-going activity. A new product must offer customers distinctive value through combination of its utility, style, price and availability. Smart companies respond, by changing their designing and developing new products. This demands a high level of creativity amongst employees.

How to Foster Creativity

Creativity is the ability to think fast, generate new ideas and deal with problems in effective ways without lose of employees zest and curiosity. A Manager continuously takes decisions in context to some task or other. If he is able to generate number of alternatives before taking his final decision, the quality of his decision will be best, brightest and high. It will be a good to the organization, if he can think of innovative systems and generate new ideas for solving problems. A creative individual is able to understand problems minutely and even see problems before others.

However, creativity value is in the development of alternatives. Normally, a employee thinks, what will the boss feel, about his initiative or idea. People discount their ideas precisely because they are their own, not of someone else. Therefore, the whole mind-set has to change. The employees must meet and express their ideas freely before the team for fair hearing. It is essential to keep the channel open and free to receive continuous flow for exchange of opinions, ideas, information and knowledge to reinforce and enrich skills. We want an accountable team to bring high-flying ideas down to earth to begin the revolution. This needs mutual trust between top-management and employees, so that new ideas popping-up from the bottom reaches to top for innovation. The creativity involves investigation of the problems in all directions, including a full understanding of what the problem is; the constraints in which it has to be solved, use of known procedures including detailed analysis etc. Few stories are quoted below for example—

(i) The Story of the Cap Vendor Part—I

Once upon a time there lived a man who made caps and sold them as he travelled from town to town. On one such tiring day as he was moving to the next town, he decided to take rest under a big banyan tree. He spread out his wares and soon fell asleep. What he failed to notice was the large number of monkeys on the tree. All the monkeys picked up the caps and donned them on their heads as the vendor was sleeping happily. The man woke up after some time and found that all his caps were missing. He had heard that monkeys do whatever you do. So he picked up a cap, put it on his head and then removed and threw it away. All the monkeys on the tree also removed their caps and threw them down. The vendor picked them up and happily proceeded to the next town. This story we have all heard. The modern version is different.

The Story of the Cap Vendor Part—II

The cap vendor became old and handed over his business to his son. His son also became old and he also handed over the business to his son. The new generation cap-vendor also moved from town to town and on one such trip, by sheer coincidence, he stopped to take rest under the same banyan tree where his grandfather had stopped decades back. The new generation monkeys waited till he fell asleep and took away all the caps like their ancestors. Our friend—the new, generation trader—had heard the story from his grandfather about how he retrieved his caps from the monkeys. So he took one cap that was left behind, put it on and then threw it away and waited for the monkeys to remove all caps and throw them away. The smart monkeys of the present generation laughed loudly, looked at our friends with contempt and said, "You think only your grandfather tells you stories!" The moral of the story is that what was good some years back may not work today. There is a need to continually think differently. Old is not always gold.

(ii) There is another story for illustration from Mahabharat. In a village, a teacher is teaching the 'Sri Krishna Janam' story to a class. The story continues . . . .

Teacher: Kansa the king of Mathura heard the forecast (Akashwani) that his sister's 8th child will kill him and he become violent . He ordered to put Vasudev and Devki in Jail. He started to kill child soon after their birth one after another.

Teacher: Students this story is from Mahabharat which everyone believe in India. Do you have any doubt?

Student: Sir, When Kansa knew that Vasudev and Devki's 8th child was going to kill him, why he did not put both of them in the separate cell to eliminate the root cause of his problem?

Teacher: Son, you are really creative. Kansa, did not take correct decision since he become short-tempered with his superpower.

(iii) A ancient story of Savitri and Satyavan is quoted below:

Princess Savitri decided to marry a poor prince Satyavan knowing well in advance that he will die after a year. After marriage, Savitri had a year time to think ahead and how to overcome the problem. After one year, Yamdoot came and took away the life of Satyavan but Savitri started chasing him all the way. Yamdoot told Savitri several times to go back but Savitri kept on following Yamdoot. Finally, Yamdoot stopped and told patiently "Why she is chasing him knowing well in advance that he cannot give back Satyavan." She replied politely "I want to be your friend." Amazingly, Yamdoot never heard such polite word in the past from any one, to be a friend of him. Yamdoot asked, "I am impressed, I will grant you one boon except the life of Satyavan. Savitri calmly replied "Please give me the boon that my in-laws can see their grand children eating in golden plates!" Yamdoot "So be it." Yamdoot started moving and Savitri was following him. Yamdoot asked "What do you want now?" Savitri "Yamdoot my in-laws are blind!" Yamdoot, "eyes given!" Again Savitri followed, Yamdoot, "Now what more." Savitri, 'they are poor." Yamdoot, "Now they are a king and a queen of a kingdom!" Savitri followed again. Yamdoot, "Now what." Savitri, "Yamdootji my in-laws have only one child. How they can have grand children!" Yamdoot, with pleasure said "Savitri, you win, go back, Satyavan is alive now!"

The moral of the story is that the power of purpose is tremendous. With purpose and persistence, practically anything is possible including creativity and innovation.

(iv) I quote here a story on 'A Lion and a Rabbit' from Panchtantra. There was a Lion in the forest who used to kill violently the animals from the forest. All the animals decide to present to the Lion, that every day one of them will come to his cave. The Lion can eat his food without any efforts.

It worked well for all, till it was the turn of the Rabbit. Rabbit started thinking in advance a better way to save his life. He found one new idea and implemented it successfully. He purposely reached late to cave and the Lion was violent-threatened dire consequences to cancel the mutual understanding. Rabbit politely told him that he was delayed by another Lion on the way and some how reached to him by long route.

The Lion lost his patience and instructed the Rabbit to take him to new Lion. Rabbit followed the instruction cunningly as per his plan and take him near a well. When the Lion looked into the well with roaring sound, he saw his own reflection with sound. Lion reacted and jumped into the well with the roaring noise. He drowned. All the animals did not believe it and told the Rabbit to show the well which he did. The animals were extremely happy due to creative thinking of the Rabbit which solved their problem forever.

Each person should recognize his own creativity as compared to others. Each person must honour and experience his own creativity; knowing that everybody else has it too. We must see the best aspect of others instead of their worst.

Styles of Creativity

(i) **MODIFYING STYLE:** Borrowing a solution from one place and implementing it into another.

(ii) **VISIONING STYLE:** Use imagination to jump into the future and make a realistic picture of how you want things to look.

(iii) **EXPLORING STYLE:** Question everything; just to see what happens as they explore.

(iv) **EXPERIMENTING STYLE:** Use the skill of making new combinations of things. It does not have a methodology and a process in mind but consider all the different opinions by creatively combining them into a solution.

Enhancing Creativity

(i) We may have to invest more of our knowledge and experience in wider search of alternatives, before we choose the best one we want.

(ii) If presence of anyone block the free expression and debate, it adversely affects the ideas generating. Techniques for encouraging creativity desires temporary removal of both internal and external censors.

How to Develop Creative Abilities

The creativity value is in the development of the alternatives. This needs the creative abilities as detailed below:

(i) Person's ability and **fluency** to come-up with a number of solutions to a given problem in a limited time.

(ii) **Flexibility** to provide a variety of solutions and use a variety of approaches from different view point in problem solving.

(iii) The ability to come-up with unusual but **originality** in appropriate responses.

(iv) The ability to identify problems i.e. the **sensitivity** even if unexplained.

(v) The ability to **identify the basic causes** of the problem and to visualise its consequences.

(vi) The ability to **elaborate on a theme.**

What Creative Traits Need to be Used

The following creative traits needs to be used:

(i) **Perceptiveness**: Being able to clearly see all the issues involved in a situation.

(ii) **Self-Concept**: The totality of attitudes, judgement and values of an individual, relating to his behaviour, abilities and qualities. Awareness of these variables and their evaluation is self concept.

(iii) **Openness**: The quality of being frank and candid in accepting other people's ideas and opinion.

(iv) **Openness to ambiguity**: An understanding that no situation is clearly defined and the acceptance of the ambiguity present in the environment.

(v) **Confidence in oneself**: Knowledge and belief in one's strength.

(vi) **A well-ordered sense of priority**: Clarity of aims and an understanding of their relative importance.

(vii) **Innovativeness:** Putting something new into practice.

(viii) **Initiative:** The ability to take action without being told by anyone.

(ix) **Divergent thinking:** The ability to think of diverse relationship.

(x) **Willingness to confront**: Fearlessness regarding consequences.

(xi) **Independence:** The ability to do a task single handedly.

(xii) **Probing:** The capacity to ask questions and examine the situation.

(xiii) **Work involvement and resourcefulness:** The ability to muster resources and devise means and ways of handling situations.

(xiv) **Risk taking:** The ability to have the courage to undertake new assignments that involve risk.

(xv) **Patience:** The ability to wait for results.

(xvi) **Ambition:** Having a desire to succeed or to achieve.

How to Manage New Product Introduction

The process of managing new product introduction is given below in phases:

(i) **Idea validation:** Defining the target customer, his unmet needs, and a new product that will meet those needs.

(ii) **Conceptual Design:** Demonstrating the marketing and manufacturing feasibility of the product.

(iii) **Specification and design:** Determining what the product will do, what it will look like and how it will be used, working out the production processes.

(iv) **Prototype production and testing**: Find out whether the product meets quality, specifications and competitive needs.

(v) **Commercialization:** Implementing the sales plan and achieving the manufacturing capacity to meet sales volume.

INNOVATION

INNOVATE TO STAY AHEAD. Innovation is getting feedback from the customers regarding their requirements and then thinking of a new product to meet those customer needs. Need is a great idea for a new, revolutionary product. Company who innovate can dominate markets. Customers need and requirement are the major source for innovation.

Our thoughts, ideas, notions, impressions and mental sensations keeps our body constantly charged through our five senses i.e. sight, hearing, touch, taste and smell. For innovation, you don't always have to start from scratch to create a winning product. New technology doesn't invariably mean high technology. Companies can prosper, even if they have no capital for pure research by exploiting the vast amounts of cheap, available technology and generating new uses for them. A **breakthrough is achieved only when two or more people are inspired, get together, have fun and think the unthinkable.** When new product is to be developed, the cross-functional teams will be reliably productive. We need to inspire people by imposing creative tension. **Speed is the element of success.**

Therefore, the following steps will be helpful to get it

done quickly, efficiently and correctly:

(i) **Make innovation the strategy**: Get top management involved, as major changes cannot occur without their commitment.

(ii) **Establish foundations**: Because innovation is impossible without knowledge and technology. The two competencies should be in place from the outset i.e. the expertise of the staff and the technological base.

(iii) **Eradicate Unsuccessful attempts:** Target for elimination the innumerable unsuccessful attempts—delays, changes, rework, and unnecessary work—that plagus most development projects.

(iv) **Put customers first:** Get more accurate information about what customers want.

(v) **Develop a business strategy:** Get the business issues right, preventing later revisions and delays.

(vi) **Design the actual product:** Product development is a complex, interconnected process involving marketing, engineering, and manufacturing. Get these groups to cooperate and to produce a fast, effective product development process.

(vii) **Improve continuously:** Ensure that the knowledge gained from doing one project is not lost but used to make the next project even more efficient.

CONCLUSION

We need to change our perceptions and concepts, so that we see things, not as they are today but as they can be tomorrow. The creative thinking looks working perfectly fine and we must try to make it still better. The best part is that this does not call for a genius.

The relation between intelligence and thinking is like the relation between a Car and a Driver. The Car's horsepower determines it's POTENTIAL, but it is the **skill of the Driver** that determines the **PERFORMANCE.** The creativity is essential for the **Survival of Business and Industry.**

"INNOVATE or PERISH" is the latest theme for survival of Industry. The necessity is **"JUST DON'T IMPROVE....... BUT INVENT."** Therefore, push strategic thinking towards consideration of new, innovative and breakthrough approaches to manage for **consistent value creation, growth and prosperity.**

PART II

"Imagination is more important than knowledge."

—*Albert Einstein*

The world is changing faster and the speed will be of the essence in every sphere. Rapid innovation, with flexible management and projected sequence of events planning will determine organisation health in the future. The world become a global village open to all. Being ethical will be even more important in the future because all prevailing rules are likely to be changed. French novelist Marcel Proust wrote,... "The real voyage of discovery consists not in seeking new lands but in seeing with new eyes."

Every organisation has to grow revenue, raise prices and cut costs. That simple arithmetic never changes. You need to bring new products and services to customers. The winners are the innovators who are making bold thinking, in everyday part of their doing business. Thinking turns experience into insight. The organisations have no option but to innovate all about products and services. In order to make innovation a core capability, the organisation must reinvent and overhaul the entire business model at regular intervals. It is equally important for organisation, not just to think of what their core competencies are but how they can borrow competencies even from other places.

How to foster innovation, fast adoption, in the face of increasing uncertainty and adversity in the market? The state of any enterprise's corporate mindset depends upon the mindset of individuals who lead the organisation. This determines.... How these individuals interact? What informations are collected? How it is processed? How decisions are made? How you respond and deal with the problems? Spontaneously change emerges, when people really believe that their voice counts. Nurture talent to develop the highest productivity. Focus on clear pre-defined outcomes, not the process. A great deal of new technology is not new knowledge, but it is new perception. It is putting together things that no one had thought of putting together before, i.e. the things that by themselves had been around us since a long time.

Both creativity and innovation has no limits. Normally, we treat creativity as a talent but idea creativity is a skill that can be learn and developed. Creativity is needed for two reasons,—one to do better than what you are doing at present and another to do different things that add more value. *Creativity is a source of inspiration and to implement effective solutions is innovation. The ability to tap the creative potential of employees and translate it into innovation, to compete on the basis of innovative products and services; make all the difference between success and failure today.* It is considered to be both a curse and a blessing, depending on how you looks at it and consequently, what course of action you adopts. The emergence of an liberalised global business environment is making our live in interesting times.

The organisation has to encourage their employees to think and think creatively. All employees have creative potential which can be harnessed and managed, so that it leads to innovation and excellence for the organisation. The successful organisation today has to reinvent itself constantly. In this process towards reinvention, everyone must contribute creatively towards enhancing organisational effectiveness, both in the present and for the future. Therefore, build an innovative mindset, arm your people with the knowledge of tools and tackles of innovation and bring in innovation at the strategy level to achieve the objectives. When got an idea, you know it will work; better put it to work, then present your superiors with the results. *The losses of creative ideas per day are incalculable because most employees do not perform as per their capacity.* Creative people have to be excited to perform at their peak. *The innovation can be the missile that companies fire to stay ahead of the competition.*

If you do not do it, the bad things will happen to you. The competition will blow you away; if you refuse to improve. Change or die. Innovate or self-destruct. Eat lunch or be lunch. Lead by example and always try to remain better to change, innovate, improve, reinvent, renew, revitalise and revolutionise. Technology that stands the test of the time to come, is the real technology.

Think creatively. Believe—it can be done. When you believe it, your mind finds ways to do it. Try new approaches. Be progressive in everything you do. Try it and see that you can do it better. Use your supreme thinking power. Use it to release your creative power. Use it to find solution to the problems. Spend some time everyday alone, just for thinking. *Doing the impossible is not really doing the impossible, but it is just doing things that other people think they can't do. Always look for opportunities rather than constraints.* Recognise your potential and exploit it. Let creativity be your guiding principle.

Once the creative idea has been identified, it must bring value to your organisation. Innovation includes the following stages:

(i) **Creativity**—The discovery of a new idea.
(ii) **Strategy**—A determination of whether the idea is new and useful.
(iii) **Implementation**—Putting the new and useful idea into action.
(iv) **Profitability**—Maximising the added value from implementation of the new and useful idea.

You must engage optimistic happy people for generating new ideas since they generate more varied ideas and combinations of those ideas exchanging assumptions of one another's. When you select people as team-members, you must examine their team innovation skills as under:

Vision

(i) Does your team have a clear vision?
(ii) Is the vision shared by all team members?
(iii) Is the vision developed and decision taken by the team members?

Participation

(i) Do team members share informations with each other?
(ii) Do team members participate in decision making process?
(iii) Are they prepared to discuss conflicting ideas with each other?
(iv) Do they share work related anxieties and achievements?
(v) Do they propose new ideas?
(vi) What methods are used to improve performance levels?
(vii) Are all members committed to excellent standards?

Support

(i) Do they support new ideas?
(ii) Do they help each other to implement new ideas?
(iii) Does the entire team offer support to new ideas?

You must be creative to initiate change for innovation. Change is a matter of perspective. If you are willing to change; look at things from a different perspective to really make the great things happen. Your expectations begin to spell your performance and your performance makes things happen.

If anything is constant in our world, it is change. Different people will have different perspectives. For timid—the change is terror; for satisfied—the change is threatening and for confident—the change spells opportunity. Keep your mind open, so that more informations are available to you to examine the matters and their alternatives.

The basic qualities needed in individuals to accept

changes for innovation are:

(i) **FLEXIBILITY**: Not occupied with the old ideas used in the past but always think for a better alternative.

(ii) **LEARNING**: Must be in constant quest for knowledge.

(iii) **OPENNESS**: A sense of openness in our minds, tells us more about what is happening around us and about us.

(iv) **WONDER**: A strong desire that with positive and affirmative changes, I can grow and become better.

(v) **EAGERNESS**: The desire to learn, grow and embrace change.

(vi) **READINESS**: Must be constantly ready to initiate and implement changes effectively, when opportunity comes our way.

Everything you do to gain pleasure or to avoid pain. Your actions and behaviour comes out of your thoughts and feelings. Most of the people change because of pain; when the pain of maintaining status—quo becomes greater than the pain of changing. Infact, you must meet the challenges of tomorrow to deliver upon commitments and share the new value. There is no choice except to embrace change, learn to live with it, capitalise upon it and celebrate the success of innovation. You should never accept the status quo but use your brain and act in a responsible manner to achieve it.

The highest organisation commitment comes through leveraging not just efforts but the minds of others. Therefore, focus to build high performance teams, developing others and taking pride and pleasure in their growth. Help other people to work on their strength to become successful. Let talent feel valued to discover their own path for achievement.

Your success depends upon your ability to innovate. For example in non-alcoholic beverages Carbonated Fountain Drink called Coca-cola was an immediate success in Atlanta area. Initially Coke sales could only grow according to the number of Soda Fountain grew. The new idea 'BOTTLE IT' changed it at all from a small regional house into an international giant company. The Coca-Cola company had the wisdom to leverage time, efforts, location by bottling their products and the rest is the history. Remember! it is not where you start but it is where you end up.

The entire world is moving and changing. We come across the opportunities, which we never thought possible. We can make things happen, we can help our organisation, we can help our people and in the process we help ourselves. We must understand that for success in management, the yesterday's ideas cannot solve the today's problems and today's ideas may not be sufficient to meet the challenges of tomorrow. The past will never come back, the future is unknown and therefore make every effort to ensure that present is the best. Improve performance continuously. Manage for value and people create value.

"You may have to fight a battle more than once to win it."

—Margaret Thatcher

PART III

Knowledge is limitless. The challenge before us is how to foster informations into knowledge and knowledge into productive use for competitive advantage. Innovation may be defined as the introduction of new knowledge for overall improvement of productivity, quality, services and delivery besides reducing costs by change in process and methods of operation. The talent, technology and time plays as driving force to utilise the identified knowledge differently to make things better for value addition.

Organisations today are undergoing the emergence of a borderless world. It's unique in many ways. Technology is being leveraged to introduce transparency and accountability in all the endeavours. Organisations surpass all limits are moving to internet, web structures, thin boundaries and virtual integration. Wealth extraction is giving way to wealth creation at speed of thought like never before. The need to lead change by performance excellence for value creation has emerged as the only way to survive and excel in the 21st century.

How to inspire ideas and innovation in the work place? Is it right way to spark creativity and encourage constructive confrontation? Winners do it differently. Creativity is the ability to come up with an idea that is novel. But creativity has no value in itself until applied with some purpose to make it happen which is known as innovation. Think in a radically different way about innovation to understand the creative process and take creative risks. Creativity and innovation can be taught, cultured and institutionalised to people of different disciplines. What works for one purpose may not work for another purpose. Therefore, we need to pick and implement the best idea matching to different purposes.

The impression that innovation is always good is not correct. Sometimes, being a fast follower has its additional advantage. Some of the companies really have no intellectual people to innovate. They look creative but infact they imitate with one another doing exactly the same thing. Therefore, you need to analyse which one is winning and follow it quickly.

While finalising an idea and making a plan is important, it is equally important that it is to be accepted by your creative team without which the final output would not match with your original thoughts. Setting expectations and earning the trust of people is really important. Better, to share what you know and learn what you don't know. Good is not good, when better is expected.

With the arrival of the World Trade Organisation regime by 2006, organisations are gearing up to face international competition. Almost all organisations have common theme to innovate for survival. You and your organisation have the goal to make money. In other words, you can express your goal; *To Increase*—the net profit, return-on-investment and cash flow. When you have a definite goal to make money, you need to work on it, physically, mentally, intellectually and whole-heartedly with self-confidence, courage, enthusiasm and strong determination in a planned manner to nurture and nourish your supreme desire.

Our minds and intellect combine together are perpetual battlefields, where our good thoughts are engaged in gaining supremacy over our evil thoughts. It is war between good values and evil tendencies. What do we do when we try to grow? We must develop virtues and techniques of destroying these evil qualities within us by showing the path to harmony, happiness, fruitfulness and prosperity. Think of best qualities in you and be totally committed to your goals. People achieve desired goals by doing things differently. As is the mind, so is the man. The goal is a steady mind where the pairs of opposite do not bother us. Action springs from ideas and those need to be planted in our minds. Allow your desires and ideas to flourish to achieve success. Surround yourself with optimist, who will be the source of keeping alive your vision, inspiration and enthusiasm to achieve your goals. Spirit is engaging our minds, hearts and souls to do the right things. Think positive and it will take you to your desired destination. We are constantly on the quest of knowledge for the next great revolution. The quest of growth is driven by the combined creativity, passion and dynamism. Victory often belongs to those who want it the most.

What's stopping you from being optimistic? Good thoughts and action can never produce bad results. Positive thinking makes winning easy. You concentrate on your core competencies. You have to convince yourself that you are the best and be committed to what you do. You must have full confidence in yourself. That's half the battle won.

The translation of an invention into a commercial application is an equally important dimension of innovation. Innovation has two important dimensions-novelty and utility, the latter proved by the acceptance from users or customers. Novelty does not necessarily mean new to the world but it can be new to a country and industry that improve efficiencies in production operation or service or delivery or quality besides reducing overall cost. The infusion of new manufacturing technologies, Kaizen, TPM and Quality

Control techniques etc. have improved productivity, quality, cost and delivery of Indian industries to innovate and compete in global market. We need to be more tolerant of experimentation which is essential elements of the innovation process. I quote here to consider the following examples:

- Bajaj Auto used to fill nearly a litre of petrol in the tanks of its motorcycles and scooters for testing the engine, mileage and overall body at its Chakkan, Pune plant, just after the assembly was completed. Not all the petrol poured into the tank was consumed; the remaining petrol had to be sucked out. Then, the idea struck. The workmen (there are no supervisors on the line) made a small metal tank that was filled with petrol and attached from outside to the engine of the motorbike under test. Once the test was over, the external tank was detached and put onto the next bike. This meant that there was no need to put petrol in the internal petrol tanks of the motorbike. The Chakkan plant makes 1,200 bikes a day. Even if a half litre of petrol is saved from every bike in this manner, that's 600 litres a day or, at the present rates of petrol, Rs 38 to a litre—nearly Rs 23,000 a day or Rs 6.8 lakh a month, i.e. Rs 82 lakh a year!
- In one of the most industrially profligate sections of Gujarat—the town of Ankleshwar—lies the well laid out manufacturing set up of the country's premier paints producer, Asian Paints. On a visit to this plant, one can find amidst the notice boards, the mention of an interesting word along with cliched manufacturing jargons like Six Sigma and quality. The word is Navsarjan—translated into English 'ushering in the new'—the Indianised equivalent of Innovation.
- Just few weeks ago, one of India's major FMCG company, Marico Industries, held an intra-company annual organisational communication exercise for its executives. One interesting theme for which some aspiring managers and their initiatives were rewarded was 'Innovation'.

- Word 'Innovation' is mentioned a dozen times in the cover itself of the FY04 annual report of Wipro. 'Innovation is Wipro', begins the cover.
- Making a low-cost Rs 5 Ice Cream, being researched in HLL laboratories, is an example of product innovation.
- Reliance, for example, has invested Rs. 150 Crore in a centre meant to do research in polyester. Reliance already holds a few patents in polyester, among them for the world's first fully black polyester fibre.
- Look at the General Elections in this year. In a span of three hours, innovation has brought about fast counting, live results updation through EVM usage. Was it the same five years back? No doubt that it is going to move on in leaps and bounds in the coming days.
- What is common to Hampstead, Universal Prime, Virgo Voyager, and Equatorial Lion? All are 11 names of Very Large Crude Carriers (VLCC) of names like Exxon Mobil Corp, Marathon Oil, Chevron Texaco or British Petroleum, a trend now catching up in India as well.

  This is happening after 4 long decades. At prevailing market rates, the use of these ships can save from \$ 0.5–\$ 1 for every barrel of crude imported. The savings on this account add to the refining margins of Indian Oil and Reliance. Both these companies have higher refining margins as compared to other players accrued from savings on logistics.

  In the '90s, India's domestic refining capacity was 65-70 million tonnes per annum (mtpa). The domestic crude oil production was in the range of 30 mtpa. Thus, the total imports were 35-40 mtpa. This scenario was altered radically after the commissioning of Reliance's 27 mtpa oil refinery at Jamnagar. At the same time, other greenfield and expansion projects took up the domestic refining capacity to 112 mtpa. As a result, crude imports into the country went up sharply allowing the use of larger ships.

A VLCC has a displacement of 200,000-320,000 dead weight tonnes (dwt) and can carry 2 million barrels of crude in a single voyage. For example an Aframax tanker is about 100,000 dwt and carries one third the load of a VLCC. At prevailing market rates, the saving on using a VLCC instead of an Aframax works out to almost $0.5/bbl for crude imports from the Persian Gulf. Big savings such as the above are the primary reasons for the shift to these ships.

Reliance, the first Indian company in using VLCCs imports some 80% of its crude requirements via these ships. Now Indian Oil, also brings in most of its crude via these ships. However since Indian ports don't have the necessary draft—water depth—Reliance and IOC use single buoy moorings (SBM) to unload these ships. Hindustan Petroleum brought in one cargo on a VLCC in June '04 and may start large-scale usage soon. Bharat Petroleum subsidiary Kochi Refineries also plans to shift over to these behemoths. VLCCs now account for about 60% of the total crude oil imported into India. The number of parcels coming into the country is 15-20 every month.

The shift is catching up also with Indian shipping companies. In the beginning of '03, there wasn't a single VLCC in the Indian shipping fleet. Around June '03, state-owned Shipping Corporation placed an order for two new building ships to be delivered by '05 other entries like Great Eastern Shipping and Essar Shipping are following suit as well. VLCCs thus seem in.

- India in the arena of technological innovation has achieved many successes. The prominent example includes that our space programme has sent a series of satellites into space that comprise the largest domestic communication system.

Success breeds success. Indian industries have made significant breakthrough in international market in areas like petro-chemicals, pharmaceuticals, computer engineering, automobiles, metals, information technology and jewellary etc. and now focus on building sustainable sources of competitiveness. The exports of Petroleum products were at a record high and expected to touched Rs. 163 billion in year 2004. Therefore, product, process and practice innovation are the important steps to aggressively build our brands image in global market. Most times, victories don't always go to the faster or stronger but to one who just believes in winning.

12

Creative Process of Problem Solving—A Satisfaction

PART I

PREAMBLE

An Organisation is the collection of employees. The success of an Organisation depends on the ability of its efficient and effective small teams of employees, within it, to work together to **attain the common goals and objectives of the total Organisation.** The members of the team must be committed to achieve the goals by involving all team members in defining the goals as well as to solve the specific problems.

Most stressful problems are really the absence of ideas. Incidentally, we can't eliminate problems unless we decide for the final exit. It cannot be solved instantly. Slowly but steadily, one by one, take care of each problem by looking for simple ideas to arrive at solutions. An idea is just an intellectual construct and requires a patience to nurture it into a reality.

When too many problems are causing you enormous stress and strain, do the followings:

(a) Think... there must be a better way to solve these

problems.

(b) Ask, ask, ask,... from yourself and from others, how to do things in better ways. Don't forget to make why-why analysis since such questions will get you intelligent and common sense answers.

(c) Creativity is a talent, all of us need to surface. Do it now. Start doing it. **Don't forget that the first step towards solving problem is to begin.** Of course, do not forget to prioritise first your problems, based upon value analysis.

They called it carbon till they realised the worth and value of diamond. Confucious said that "Just as diamond does not shine without being sharpened with pressure, one cannot become a complete person without experiencing difficulties."

OBJECTIVES OF PROBLEM SOLVING (FOR EXAMPLE)

(a) Improvement of overall quality of work life.

(b) Improvement of product Q.C.D. i.e. quality, cost and delivery.

APPROACH TO PROBLEM SOLVING

"There is always scope for improvement" should pervade the entire organisation. Basically, a questioning mind is a prerequisite for problem solving. The six best friends in solving problems are **"WHAT, WHY, WHEN, WHERE, WHO and HOW"**. These should be effectively used to question the **PURPOSE, PLACE, PERSON, SEQUENCE and METHOD OF OPERATIONS.** Coupled with this questioning mind, a creative outlook is required. Once a problem is identified and feasible solutions generated, the attitude should be to enthusiastically implement, instal and maintain it, if the solution is effective.

CREATIVE PROCESS OF PROBLEM SOLVING AND DECISION MAKING

The problem solving and making decisions are two critical team functions. If a group proposes to improve its ability to function as a team, the proper methods for solving problems and making decisions should be adopted. **Remember ! to solve important problems now, before they become cronic and urgent.** The lack of agreed approaches can result in waste of time, misunderstandings, frustration and more importantly "Bad decisions".

In order to achieve zero breakdowns and to eliminate all chronic losses affecting productivity, manpower efficiency, material, power (energy); certain systematic structural tools and techniques are required.

The stages involved in problem solving are **PLAN, DO CHECK** and **ACTION.** Each project will have to pass through four stages and then a new project is taken up in the same way.

For systematic approach, a guideline in brief regarding creative process of problem solving are given below in seriatim.

STEP	PLAN
(1)	Identify and select the specific problem to be solved. Ensure that it solves the problem which **the organisation considers most significant.**
(2)	Establish the theme.
(3)	Assemble an effective problem solving group to ensure interdependence between members.
(4)	Problems should be welcomed as an opportunity, since they help us to focus the search, for discovering the improvements.
(5)	Brainstorming to produce ideas and a steady flow of suggestions for improvement.
(6)	Challenge your situations, assumptions and define what need to be done. Develop criteria or specify goals.
(7)	Gather relevant data and ensure that it is quantifiable.

STEP	PLAN
(8)	Plan the schedule and activities to achieve the objective in minimum time, within available resources.
(9)	Understand the current situation.
(10)	Set the target.
	DO
(11)	Investigate the problem.
(12)	Establish the target.
(13)	Analyse the cause of the problem.
(14)	Generate possible solutions and think for alternatives available for solving the problem or courses of action.
(15)	Evaluate the alternatives in the light of the data and the objectives of the team. Data enhances decisiveness, analytical skill and bridges the unknown to nurtures the innovation and development.
(16)	Think, select and plan for ideal solution. Assess specific benefits like cost reduction, streamline operations, improve our image with our customers etc.
(17)	Analyse the constraints.
(18)	Breakdown the departmental barriers, blocking path to improvement and obstructing impartial decision. The problems should be solved on the basis of what is best for the organisation as a whole, rather than any sectional interest.
(19)	Look for optimal creative solution.
(20)	Define criteria for making decision.
(21)	Make the decision.
	CHECK
(22)	Confirm the results.
	ACTION
(23)	Standardise the action.
(24)	Action to implement the decision.
(25)	Check the result and evaluate solution, that it has worked.
(26)	Plan to eliminate the causes before the problem actually happens.
(27)	Review and continuously improve.

CONCLUSION

The various steps cannot be used like a water tight compartment but should be used as a need based requirement suited to solve the specific problems. To enhance creativity, i.e. effectiveness of problem solving, it is better to work in groups like -Quality Circles, Quality Improvement Teams, Cross Functional Teams etc. It is a verified fact that the ideas generated by people working in groups are much better in quality and quantity than those of individuals. This is so, because people can build better on the ideas of others.

The team leader have to keep monitoring the system. The effective team will be shared and supported by all the members to decide the above process with suitable variations to attain the common goals of the Organisation.

Innovation, Expertise, Creativity, Empathy, Metaphysics and Problem Solving Skills are the competitive edge for tomorrow that emerges for today. Therefore, **it is essential to find the answers today for tomorrow's problems.** REMEMBER! SUCCESS IS A JOURNEY AND NOT A DESTINATION WHICH IS THE RESULT OF RIGHT DECISIONS WITHIN THE RIGHT TIME.

PART II

INTRODUCTION

If we really want improvements, we should never accept the status quo but find problems to solve them. The slogan **"ELIMINATE WASTE"** is posted in many plants, I have visited. But as long as someone knows that something constitutes waste, he will eliminate it. The real problem is not noticing, something which is really wasteful. Therefore, the slogan ought to be **"FIND WASTE"**. The systematic thinking for improvement combines the following stages:

IDENTIFY PROBLEMS

Never accept the status quo. Find problems, where you

think no problem exist. You must be dissatisfied with the status quo—always ask why productivity cannot be increased? Why stocks maintained are necessary? Can we find better ways to improve things? Can you make use of our creative thinking power to solve the complex problems? For instance, I would like to cite following examples.

(I) As per Ramayana, Hanumanji was famous as problem solver, courageous, sharp mind, intelligent and for imagination, initiative, sincerity, loyalty and faithfulness. Once the life of Laxmana was in danger and therefore Rama sent Hanumanji to bring 'Sanjeevani Bunti' and also Vaidhya Susen. When Hanumanji reached the mountain, he could not identify Sanjeevani. Hanumanji had neither seen Sanjeevani nor the full specification was given to him. The latest communication system like phone, fax, E-mail and internet were not at all in existance at that time, to obtain relevant information. Hanumanji neither asked the questions nor came back to Rama for obtaining details keeping in view the emergency of the work. Hanumanji used his supreme thinking power to solve this complex problem. As per his creative thinking, he picked up the mountain 'Dronachal' and flew back with it, hoping that Sanjeevani was growing on it. Similarly, he brought the Vaidhya Susen, even along with his house, from Sri Lanka. Thus Hanumanji did the work to save the life of Laxmana. Like a Rama and a Hanumanji, we all must take inspiration to solve the complex problems to achieve the success.

(II) Another prominent example includes that during Sri Lanka war both Rama and Laxmana were tied up in Snake knot by Ravana. All the Generals of Rama side were in complex problem and they were not in a position to suggest any workable solution. At that time, Hanumanji used his supreme thinking power to brought Garudji for this purpose and achieved success to destroy snake knot. Similarly, we must also use our creative thinking power to resolve the critical problems.

APPLY BASIC APPROACH TO IMPROVEMENT

(i) UNDERSTAND THE STATUS QUO: The most magnificent improvement scheme in the world will be worthless, if we have a wrong perception of the current situation. Think, either we do not try to grasp the real facts or ignore changes that occur over-time.

(ii) PERSUE GOALS: The goals for improvement must be to make things easier, better, faster and cheaper. Therefore, (a) Focus on the goals, (b) Recognize multiple goals, (c) Persue goals systematically, and (d) Work gradually towards higher goals.

(iii) FIND BETTER MEANS: No improvement could be possible, if we just have a single means to an end. Think for multiple means or alternatives to make further improvements possible. We should consider our goals vigorously from various perspectives to discover more means and better methods.

MAKE PLANS FOR IMPROVEMENT

When we are not satisfied with the way a job is performed, we look in on a problem and ask why a particular method is used? In such cases, brainstorming is essential to entertain doubts, formulate criticisms, find reality and generating the means of responding to goals.

PUT IMPROVEMENT PLANS INTO PRACTICE

The excellent improvement plans in the world will be ineffective unless they are put into practice. Therefore, improvement must proceed through following steps:

(i) Discuss the need for improvement and set the action.
(ii) Discuss among active teams to decide on suggestions for improvement.
(iii) Determine the broad themes of improvements,
(iv) Discuss how ideas should be brought up.
(v) Present suggestions for improvement.

MAINTAIN CONSISTENT BUSINESS SUCCESS

YOU LOVE TO SOLVE PROBLEMS. YOU ARE FASCINATED BY IDEAS. Discover your strengths. We need to start with employee's current strengths and values, potential future role, gap in skills, coaching and monitoring requirements. Everybody has certain talents and strengths with a combination of knowledge and experience. Identify talent in the organisation with desired skills and competencies. **"If you are naturally gifted at music but poor at sports, the time spent learning music might make you a world—class musician. But time spent practising sports will at the best make you an average sports person. So why to waste your time on sports?"** We must keep the category of REAL TALENT clearly identified for specific jobs. It's talented people will be our biggest assets for consistent business success. I quote here a story the moral of which is that experience counts.

Christopher Columbus was stranded in Jamaica for want of supplies. He knew that an eclipse was due to occur the next day. He told the tribal chief. "The God who protects me will punish you. Unless you give me supplies that night, a vengeance will fall upon you and the moon shall lose its light." When the eclipse darkened the sky, Columbus got all the desired supplies.

In the early 1900s, an Englishman tried the same trick on a Sudanese Chieftain. "If you do not follow my order," he warned, "Vengeance will fall upon you and the moon will lose its light." The Sundanese Chieftain replied, "If you are referring to the lunar eclipse, that doesn't happen until the day after tomorrow."

PART III

Are you tired of running your Business/Industry with outdated practices? If you find the difficulty in each problem, we will make you find the solution for every problem. Knowledge is power. Learning is a serious business because our success depends on it. Therefore, to become the best, our knowledge should be the best in the world. Through the knowledge of all tasks and faster decisions; you can now save your time to focus on more important matters. Thus make your industry/business more efficient, effective and successful with excellent solutions to each problem. 'Many men, many minds and good mind, good find' is a universal fact. Man does not see with his eyes alone, but he also sees with the mind which penetrate into visibility and understand things as clearly as he sees with his eyes.

Business is run to provide the products and services for utmost satisfaction of customers with an objective to generate wealth for organisation and shareholders. Normally to achieve it, we have to solve problems but problems demand creativity to implement a solution which has a long lasting effect. Therefore, an organisation has to provide an environment of confidence/belief, faith/trust, values, work culture, pride, synergy and self-discipline to recognise the nature of problem and develop a solution. If you have a will to achieve it, nothing is impossible. It's a matter of how you plan your competence! You can win even if you don't have the capacity but have a strong will and foresight to achieve unprecedented success by pooling resources and implementing new ideas to become action oriented. You need to realise the full potential of your business and harness your core competencies.

CLASSIFICATION OF PROBLEMS

The problems have life cycles that can be classified into three categories:

(i) IMPORTANT STAGE: In this stage, the problem has no immediate threat. It would be equivalent to your car having a low level of oil in it. You can still drive the car for a while and once you fill more oil in your car, the problem would be solved. It is an important stage in problem solving since it is not an immediate threat.

(ii) EMERGENT STAGE: In this stage, the problem is

more than a minor nuisance since some damage has already been done. That would be like driving your car with a worn-out bearing. If you don't change the bearing, your car will break-down. Since damage has already been done, you need to pay close attention to replace the bearing in your car at the earliest.

(iii) CRISIS STAGE: In this stage, the problem is life threatening to the organisation and if this problem is not solved, the organisation could cease to function effectively. That will be equivalent to driving your car on a very busy highway with no oil or very little oil, with the heat temperature very high and smoke coming out of your engine. It is crisis stage and you may face break-down since the car may stop functioning.

The easiest stage which should be taken care of is at the important stage in which you can solve problem and move on. The resource demanded will not have to be heavy and great. Once the problem gets to the emergent stage, it becomes more complicated and at the crisis stage, who knows if it could even be solved to any satisfactory position. Therefore, you need to become more mindful, to solve today's problem with tomorrow's solutions.

Therefore, involve people, brain-storm for their suggestions, obtain their opinions, select the best solution and allow people to implement it. Since it is a group decision, people are committed to it, they believe in it, they are much more likely to follow it to make things happen. Mobilise all the brain-power to solve the significant problems being faced by organisation. Use insight in result based innovation and lineup vision in strategic thinking, passion, continuous improvement, collaborative teamwork in creation, sharing and application of knowledge through continued learning combined with experience. Always think in advance to implement solution properly, effectively and consistently. Coming together of people, ideas, resources and systems makes all the difference in over-all results. Success does not mean you don't have problems. It means that you are genius and know how to solve problems.

PART IV

"The true, strong and sound mind, is the mind that can embrace equally great things and small."

— *Samuel Johnson*

WELCOME PROBLEMS AS THE SOURCE OF IMPROVEMENT

- Where no problem is perceived there can be no improvement.
- Question everything we do.
- Breakdown barriers, blocking path to improvement.
- See problems as mountains of treasure.

TACTS OF PROBLEM SOLVING

Remember, to use the following pearls of wisdom during problem solving; wherever appropriate.

(i) **OPTIMIST:** Be optimist. "Man is the master of his destiny." The person who expects the best in life and sees the good even in the bad, realising that in adversity as well as opportunity; there is some thing to be gained. Optimist are simply people who have learned how to discipline their attitudes of mind to their advantage. Mount Everest was conquered and man landed on moon with an optimist positive attitude. It is all about perseverance and persistence. It is an acquired mental skill.

(ii) **OPEN MIND:** This implies a mind that is not prejudiced, pre-set, confused or caught in the experience of the past. OPEN MIND is like a room having many windows so that the breeze and the winds can blow from all sides and directions; keeping curiosity alive, seeking desired knowledge.

The *Bhagawad Gita*, Chapter 4, text 39 says —

श्रद्धावॉल्लभते ज्ञानं तत्पर: संयतेद्रिय:।
ज्ञानं लब्ध्वा परां शान्तिमचिरेणाधिगच्छति।।

A faithful man who is dedicated to surpass knowledge and who overpower his senses, is eligible to achieve such knowledge; and having achieved it, he quickly attains the supreme peace.

जो कर्म-तत्पर है, जितेन्द्रिय और श्रद्धावान है।
वह प्राप्त करके ज्ञान, पाता शीघ्र शान्ति महान् है।।

The *Bhagawad Gita*, Chapter 5, text 16 says —

ज्ञानेन तु तदज्ञानं येषा नाशितमात्मन:।
तेषामादित्यवज्ज्ञानं प्रकाशयति तत्परम्।।

When, however, one is enlightened with the knowledge by which ignorance is destroyed, then his knowledge reveals everything, as the sun lights-up everything in the daytime.

पर दूर होता ज्ञान से, जिसका हृदय - अज्ञान है।
करता प्रकाशित 'तत्व', उनका ज्ञान सूर्य समान है।।

We should be able to adopt the best from the rest of world. Therefore, we must listen with interest to what others have to say rather than being pre-occupied with individual's own views and opinion. The ego of individual harm the organisation. Egos often make managers close-minded. If an individual is given enough exposure of inter-disciplinary work and is a member of cross-functional team, in due course of time, he may develop respect for others, their work and their abilities.

(iii) **PRODUCTIVITY:** Productivity is, above all, a state of mind. It is an attitude that seeks the continuous improvement than what exists. It is a conviction that one can do better today than yesterday and that tomorrow will be more better than today. It constantly upgrade our skills, technology, machines and people to deliver our customers the best. It eliminates the activities which waste time and money instead of adding value. It plans ahead to eliminate the slightest possible error by doing it right the first time and every time.

What is productivity common sense? Productivity can be termed as total outputs of the organisation as compared to total inputs used. The options to improve the outputs in relation to inputs are given below in seriatim of preference.

(a) Increase the output, while decreasing the input.

(b) Make the output larger, for the same input.

(c) Make the input smaller, for the same output.

(d) Make the same output of value-added product, for the same input.

(e) Increase the output faster, than the input increases.

(f) Decrease the output less, than the inputs decrease.

We need to think always to improve the quality, productivity, delivery and to reduce the product cost. Never be satisfied. Strive constantly to improve the product and reduce the rejects / waste. Inspire everyone to find ways to do everything better. Feel proud on improved achievements and communicate, how it will benefit to all.

(iv) **QUALITY:** Quality is always important since it works as a driving force in the market place. Quality results to make money, by reducing cost and making the products or services more attractive in the market place. Less money is leaking out and more is coming in. It results in loyal customers. Loyal customers will buy again and bring their friends to buy the products. If the product or service meets or exceeds, a customer's expectations, time and time again, then in the mind of that customer; it is quality product or service. The cost is long forgotten but quality is remembered forever.

Quality Control is the art of battle on errors. We need tools to fight the battle. We have many tools in Quality Control to identify, analyze and isolate problems. We also need techniques to get data, ideas for involving people who can participate in the process. Hence, the technique of Brain Storming is a very powerful aid in the subject of Quality Management. People forget how fast you did a job, but they will remember how well you did it. The quality standard can never be static but the continuous quality improvement is the only alternative to satisfy the customers need. The quality is not the absence of defect but the presence of value in customer's eye. Remember, "Trivial, Trivial, makes perfection and perfection is not trivial."

छोटी छोटी बातों से पूर्णता आती है,
और पूर्णता कोई छोटी बात नहीं।

Besides, the continuous quality improvement leads to excellence in productivity.

(v) **BRAIN STORMING:** Brain Storming is a means of getting a large number of ideas from a group of people in a short time. It brings out, the ideas trapped in people's minds. It is not the people with money but the ideas come first. It is an idea generating technique, in which a group of people throw out their ideas as they think of them, so that each has the opportunity to build on the ideas of others. The problem should be understood clearly by everyone and the ideas that group members give should be brief and specific. An atmosphere of freedom should be encouraged. People with new ideas win in the end.

Many times, ideas are locked up some where in the

mind and not reflected at the right time. Effort is required to bring it out. Creative thinking uses ideas which are already in existence within the minds of people.

Persons close to the job, knows the best about their job and should have an opportunity to contribute. This provides an opportunity for all to participate in a creative way.

(vi) **COLLECTIVE WISDOM:** The effectiveness of an organisation depends on ability to use the collective wisdom of all. No individual alone can be expected to have a capacity and talent to solve all complex problems. Therefore, it becomes essential to functionally pool the collective knowledge, experience, skills, intelligence and creativity of a group of individuals by attitudes of cooperation, respect of others, giving credit to others for their contribution, respect for experience as well as a general belief that two brains are better than one. This can be effectively used only when all the people concerned with the process are fully involved. The evidence strongly suggests that a consensus approach yield more creative decisions and more effective implementation as compared to individual decision making. Organisation of the future must rely more upon commitment to the participative problem - solving—process instead of submission to command authority.

CREATIVE THINKING helps to gather many ideas and **ANALYTICAL THINKING** consolidate and focus on solutions. Though these two types of thinkings are different, yet they are linked, since one type complements the other.

]THINKING

ANALYTICAL	CREATIVE
(a) Logic	Imagination
(b) Unique (Few)	Many Possible.
(c) Ideas/Answers	Ideas/Answers
(d) Convergent	Divergent
(e) Verticle	Lateral

(vii) **SPEED OF RESPONSE:** We have to transform our organizations rapidly in response to a fast changing competitive business environment. Progressive and competitive organizations would not only make the right decision but it would necessarily make them faster, quicker and speedier than its competitors. Low speed of reaction and inordinate delay in decision may adversely affects the results. Therefore, it is essential that we are highly responsive and manned by competent and committed individuals. High speed of response demands full concentration, upto date information base and the ability to take calculated risk. The recent expectation on speed of response is too high because of technological advancement and the internet.

The market is changing rapidly and slow decision-making is really a big problem. Responsiveness is viewed as the key organisational competency but only few believe they have it. We need to expand the business but this needs a whole other set of skills. People will define the speed at which a organisation can adopt to change. There are several segments which offers substantial growth opportunities. The challenge before us is to be able to manage and build upon these opportunities. There is no doubt that if our reaction speed falls behind, we will stand no where in the international competition. Therefore, we need to develop our organisational capability and swiftness to absorb this growth opportunity.

(viii) **CREATE SOLUTION TO PROBLEMS** EVEN IN **IMPOSSIBLE SITUATIONS:** Darwin's "Survival of the fittest" has been at work since the origin of the universe. The power of our creator are inherent in all of us. When we are faced with impossible situations, we need only to adopt an active, assertive response. We must have faith in ourselves and in our natural inborn abilities and use creative thinking to come up with solutions to the problems. When we actively, consciously ponder on possibilities, our subconscious mind will automatically create the solutions. Our faith energises this process. Try to find the opportunity in every difficulty. Victory goes to the courageous.

(ix) **SHARED VISION:** Shared vision refers to a single image in which large number of people within the organisation are involved to acknowledge, understand and draft it. All employees within the business set up must understand, share and contribute to convert their common vision into reality.

(x) **CONTINUOUS IMPROVEMENT:** An organisation where everyone is making improvement has "TOTAL EMPLOYEES INVOLVEMENT". It constitutes non-stop improvement which can be sustained in long run only by group decision making in the organisational working. The corporate culture of Indian Industries also demands, search for different areas, with more openness towards the scope for improvement by collective wisdom.

This process shall aim at:

- Elimination of all losses affecting productivity, quality, manpower efficiency, materials and power.
- Improvement of overall equipment effectiveness.
- Use of problem solving tools to eliminate chronic defects and imperfections methodically.
- Systematically return in equipments and production line, similar to the performance standard of "new" equipment.

- Involving all employees in improvement activities. Achieving full automation and unmaned production systems.
- Reducing cost.
- Improving ease of operation and safety.
- Respecting and implementing in-house ideas and innovations.
- Achieving zero breakdowns in equipment and production lines.

Constant but continuous efforts in the right direction, to set things right through involvement of people in teams, is the theme of continuous improvements. Continuous improvement projects are identified and implemented by teams well coordinated with top management.

Improvement Proposals

Improvement Proposal welcomes any employee to come out with constructive ideas in any area of business. Proposals are invited on any topic which can add value to the organization. These proposals are evaluated by a team of top level executives of the organization. The number of proposals expressed by an employee is an indication of the motivation level of the employee.

The benefits of Improvement Proposals are many:

- Employees will be able to contribute their constructive ideas on any function of business.
- They draw on everyone's capability to think and rethink to better the product and service to the customer.
- Constructive proposals from employees can contribute to the improved health of the organization.
- Ideas generated in-house tend to be more self-sustaining.
- Employees feels proud of their workplace when they see their ideas to work in practice.

Increased motivation levels can foster team activities.

Classic innovation and the continuous improvement differ widely:

Continuous Improvement	*Innovation*
* Values the process	* Values the result
* Small steps	* Big Steps
* Current know-how	* Technological breakthrough
* Applied effort	* Cash investment
* Slow growth economy	* Fast growth economy
* Low risk	* High risk

We must value BOTH, the Process and the Result.

13

Cost Reduction Programme —Profitable Ventures

All costs are unnecessary until and unless proven otherwise. Inspired by "A RUPEE SAVED IS A RUPEE EARNED" is exactly what need to be done in the Cost Reduction Programme (CRP). The theme is to improve the Quality of product or Service, while reducing the cost. Employees are encouraged to form Cross Functional teams and highlight an area wherein they can assure the Company of saving. This can be achieved by empowering each employee through motivation and sense of teamwork. Such programme creates a culture of savings and a sense of belonging in the collective mindset of the workforce. The questions arise:

* What are tactics for surviving in the downturn or tough competition and long term strategies for winning in future?
* What are the smarter moves for tougher time?

The manufacturing involves to improve quality and reduce inventory and cost resulting in increase of profitability and productivity. For instance, appropriate manufacturing is derived from the philosophy that "INVENTORY IS EVIL." "The Total Quality Control (TQC) system is based on doing it right the first time." Kaizen, or nonstop productivity improvement comes from the philosophy "THERE IS ALWAYS A BETTER WAY." The cost reduction movement is based on the belief that "COST IS POTENTIAL PROFIT."

WHAT ARE THE REASONS FOR HIGH COST

People make mistakes, miss-targets and show lack of capacity. Often they don't achieve their targets. Morale is low and time killing as well as absenteeism are part of the prevailing culture. The wasted working time, low productivity, inadequate planning, ineffective day-to-day supervision, lack of concentration on under-performers are some of the basic reasons of high cost. Even small changes can yield improvements by engaging talented people with exceptional achievements, skills, abilities and experience in each area to manufacture the best quality at down-to-earth price. Thus we need to make every employee to cut costs. The high cost can certainly be prevented but who has the next big idea? We need to put productivity at the top of list to keep organisation competitive.

We have to ensure that the best—selling products should address universal needs and adapt to make customers more comfortable. Therefore, we should start small and expand gradually on cost reduction programme. In order to achieve it, we must eliminate the waste. How to identify the waste? Waste can be ascertained only by asking two simple questions i.e. one 'Whether the additional process will contribute to the functional value of end product?' and second 'Is customer is willing to pay extra for additional process?' If answer to any one is in YES that means it is a VALUE—ADDED—ACTIVITY. If answer to both the questions are in NO that means it is WASTE.

The success in future will largely depend on creating lowest cost product with high value addition in quality to achieve unprecedented growth.

Lower the Cost is Profit

A company is cost-conscious by treating all costs as

potential profit and cost increase becomes "PROFIT THAT IS LOST."

The traditional way of looking at cost is based on the equation:

SALES = COSTS + PROFITS.

In other words, cost is a given value to which you add whatever profit you want to make to get the selling price.

The world-class cost outlook is based on the equation:

PROFITS = SALES – COSTS.

This is mathematically equivalent to the first one, but philosophically different. From this second perspective, cost is anything that you deduct from sales and reduces your profit. In other words, any cost could have been profits, or PROFITS = SALES if cost is zero. This novel view of costs as potential profits is a philosophy that guides many companies in cornering and competing in international markets.

Let us again reflect on the two equations:

(1) SALES = COST + PROFITS
(2) PROFITS = SALES – COSTS

Take two companies, company X, a typical company that espouses formula 1, and company Y, a world-class company that lives by formula 2. Both will launch a new product in the market. Let's simulate, how they might differ in approach.

Company X will start by getting the production cost estimate—raw material, labour, overhead, etc. Then its management will decide how much margin to make on the new product based on past experience or overall corporate profit goals. Finally, it will set the selling price and start selling.

Company Y will start by asking the customer how much he is willing to pay for the new product. The company does not question nor bargain with the desired price given by the customer who is assumed to be always right. Then company Y asks its manufacturing people how much the new product would cost. Profit (or loss) is eventually derived as the final step; sales of the new product begins if profit is appropriate as determined by management.

For company Y, sales, an independent variable, is not a result of any calculation, but is a given value—given by the customer. Also, profit, a dependent variable, is not decided or given by anybody, not even by management; profit is the consequence or result of what is given by the customer—sales and what decided by the company's efforts—cost.

Which of the two companies makes more profit? Assume both companies will launch a new type of ball pen. Company X estimates its production cost at Rs. 10/-; its management decides to make a profit of Rs. 2/- so the company tries to sell the pen at Rs. 12/- a piece. Company Y starts by asking customers for how much they would buy the proposed pen. The customers say that they would be willing to pay only Rs. 9.50 for such a pen. Then Company Y asks its manufacturing people how much it would cost to make such a pen, given Rs. 9.50 as market price. The factory accepts the challenge. With its best efforts, using Kaizen, value analysis and value engineering, productivity techniques, etc. it can produce the pen at Rs. 9/-. At Rs. 0.50 profit per pen, the management of company Y decides to go ahead, launch the product and start selling it.

Question: How much profit will company Y make per pen? Rs. 0.50. Right. How much will company X make? Rs. 2/-. Wrong. Company X will make zero profits, since all the customers will buy from Company Y which sells the pen at the lower price. For company X, sales and profit are zero and imagined. Only its cost is real. For company Y, everything is real—sales, cost, and most of all, profit. At this point, company X folds up or may go into other businesses.

To be Price-Competitive becomes Cost-Competitive

But the war is not over yet—company Y has only won a battle. With a big initial sales volume that results economies of scale, and with Kaizen and non-stop cost-reduction, production costs starts to decline, say, to Rs. 8.50. They can keep the price at Rs. 9.50 and now make more profit, Rs. 1/- per pen. Kaizen continues, costs continue to decrease—this time to Rs. 8/-. The company can now start lowering its price to Rs. 9/- and still make a profit of Rs. 1/- per piece. Customers are happier, and more competitors fold up because none can sell at Rs. 9/- per pen.

As Kaizen and quality improvement continue, good things continue to happen to company Y: costs go down, profits continue to increase, sales and market share rise until virtually all competitors disappear. Their ultimate secret, is their costs. We only know the price they offer, but we cannot use our own costs as reference because their costs are much lower. Lower costs give them the power to price marginally, such that they make money on the sheer volume generated by their lower prices.

Cost competitiveness is price competitiveness. Low cost is a marketing weapon, that gives your sales force the freedom and flexibility to match or beat competitors in a price war. Conversely, high cost ties the hands of your sales force and serves as a severe handicap, especially in competitive markets in which they have to make on-the-spot price decisions to clinch a sale. Low cost puts the company in a no-lose situation and its competitor in a no-win one. A cost-superior company can price low—which its competitors cannot match—but still earn some profits. In the absence of competition, it can maximize profits by pricing as high as the market can bear.

Cost Reduction is Better than Sales Increase

A short exercise demonstrates—the power of cost reduction. In terms of profitability, which is better—a 10% increase in sales or a 10% reduction in cost? Think your answer before proceeding any further.

Take a hypothetical company A with sales of Rs. 100, cost equal to Rs. 70, and therefore, Rs. 30 profit. Assume that it is a single—product company, price is uniform, and all costs are basically variable. Let us now look at two scenarios.

	Current	*10% Sales increase*	*10% Cost decrease*
Sales	100	110	100
Cost	70	77	63
Profit	30	33	37
% Profit increase		10%	23%

Suppose another company B, has costs equal to Rs. 90. Let's see the results of the two scenarios:

	Current	*10% Sales increase*	*10% Cost decrease*
Sales	100	110	100
Cost	90	99	81
Profit	10	11	19
% Profit increase		10%	90%

This illustrates several enlightening conclusions. A reduction in cost improves profitability much better than an increase in sales. A sales increase will increase profit only by the same percentage—10% in both companies. However, a cost reduction will increase profit by more than the percentage cost was reduced i.e. more than 10% in both cases.

COST IS THE GOLD MINE IN ANY COMPANY'S **BACKYARD** that we fail to see because the paradigm that costs fixed and uncontrollable blocks our view. A concerted effort to reduce cost or even save off a few percentage points -1% reduction may even do—will go a long way towards profits.

This is not a call to stop all marketing efforts; it is a call to give the same concern and efforts we give to cost reduction as we give to marketing. Doing both simultaneously would be ideal; cost reduction effects on profits are multiplied by the sales volume generated by marketing efforts.

Cost Increase is Worse than Sales Decline

As you may have suspected, **COST IS A DOUBLE-EDGED SWORD.** It can jack up profit or squash it. If cost is left unmanaged, it rises rapidly. The effect of cost increase is the exact reverse of cost reduction. Any cost increase will have a more disastrous effect on profits than sales decline of the same percentage. Furthermore, the higher your cost component, the greater the negative effects of cost increase. The following illustration based on the previous example shows this other character of cost.

Company A

	Current	*10% Sales decrease*	*10% Cost increase*
Sales	100	90	100
Cost	70	63	77
Profit	30	27	23
% Profit decrease		-10%	-23%

Company B

	Current	*10% Sales decrease*	*10% Cost increase*
Sales	100	90	100
Cost	90	81	99
Profit	10	9	1
% Profit decrease		-10%	-90%

In view of the above, most of the companies have experienced that cost increase can wipe out profits faster than a sales decline of the same magnitude. **COST REDUCTION IS A MUST, NOT AN OPTION, FOR SURVIVAL.** Through continuous cost reduction, they make sure their marketing efforts result not only in a sale, but in a profitable sale.

How to Reduce Costs

The few areas to reduce the cost are given below:

(i) The Big Value Items

Concentrate on the big value items. They are always few in number that really matters but may contribute upto seventy percent of the total cost. Thus your efforts will produce worthwhile results.

(ii) Hidden Costs

Search and eliminate the miscellaneous or hidden costs which includes like DELAYS, BREAKDOWNS, FRUSTRATIONS and LOSS OF PRODUCTION etc. This results in large increase of expenditure which are usually scattered under different accounting heads.

(iii) Machine Breakdown Cost

We must keep the smooth flow of continuous production. Machine breakdown and anything else that hinders the flow of production must be dealt with immediately since this involve heavy depreciation cost, interest, wages of the operators of the machine, expensive service, loss of profit and upset caused in other sections due to non-availability of the part which was to be produced from breakdown machine.

(iv) Cost of Obsolete Equipment

Use of absolute equipment usually results for more expensive cost than if one had modern upto-date but costlier equipment. This reflects in quality as well as quantity of the product.

(v) Idle Time of Machine and Man Cost

This results in huge increase in production cost.

(vi) Cost of Movement

The cost of movement in an organisation can be enormous. That is why the lay-out of a factory and the movement of material have to be very carefully examined. A little extra thinking may save huge amount provided the lay-out and flow of work is organised in such a manner that movement is reduced to the minimum.

(vii) Buying

Buying is important since purchase of goods and materials involves over 60% of the selling price. It is not the cheapest price alone that matters but the reliability of product, availability of spares and the frequency of breakdowns. When you make a purchase, the core concerns to be taken into account are followings:

(a) Have you ever persued an initiative which can cut purchase cost by 10 to 15 per cent?

(b) Do you understand your supplier's economics and discuss with them what should be the cost?

(c) Do you re-evaluate your supplier's base to explore better price?

(d) Does your purchasing function, attracts the highest performing managers, within your company, to suggest further improvements?

A Quick-Hit Approach to Cost Reduction

The best and brightest ideas adopted by some of the industries for a quick-hit approach to cost reduction are given below:

(i) Eliminate unproductive practices and procedures first.

(ii) Switch-off undesired Air Conditioners.

(iii) Lay-off the extra employees or create alternative jobs for them.

(iv) Reduce inventory.

(v) Travelling of Senior Executives in economy class Air.

(vi) Video Conferencing to Cut travel cost.

(vii) Stop stay of guests in costly hotels but to put them in companies guest houses.

(viii) Print ordinary annual reports instead of premium

reports with glossy paper and fancy look.

(ix) Publish Quarterly/Annual Reports in only one main Newspaper compared to 5 to 6 Newspapers.

(x) Reduce telephone bills.

(xi) Improve efficiency and develop a will to win. Inspire and encourage willingness of your employees to do the assigned tasks with interest and enthusiasm. Also provide enrichment in skills and competencies of employees to deliver results.

(xii) Reduce power and fuel costs.

(xiii) Stop work that makes no sense and does not contribute directly to improve efficiency, effectiveness, productivity, quality, value, customer satisfaction, employees benefit and profit.

(xiv) Avoid all repetition of work.

(xv) Outsourcing business operations to cut costs.

(xvi) The ability to negotiate effectively is a core management competency.

The success of individuals and their organisations depends on their improved influencing negotiation skills.

Cost Transparent

Companies seldom realize that as long as the customer gets the right quality at the right time at a price that is reasonable, he doesn't care about your costs and profits. As long as he gets value for money, he doesn't care if you make 5% or 100% profit, or whether your cost is 99% or 5% of price. In other words, he will keep on buying as long as he perceives, he is getting the expected value from his purchase. Unlimited cost reduction and profitability must continue as long as you do not compromise quality and product delivery.

What are the strategic implications of cost transparency and cost-as-profit outlook? The cost is not inherent in the product or the industry. With their continuous cost reduction programs, rather than be affected by industry norms and practices, they affect and pull down industry cost standards. They become the cost leaders in the industry, and eventually also the price leaders.

To a company, there are no such things as fixed, uncontrollable, or given costs. A huge part of these "untouchable" costs are really unnecessary costs due to mistakes and bad decisions made in the past that have continued as standards. Now company assumes that all costs are controllable, preventable, or reducible. This belief is what drives them to do continuous improvement.

The most important implication is that all costs are unnecessary unless proven otherwise. This goes several steps beyond zero-based budgeting—to zero based costing. In other words, for cost reduction, the floor is the limit. The aim is zero cost—an allied objective of zero defects and zero inventory. If you set the floor as the limit for your costs, then the sky will be the limit for your profits. It is common to see that companies achieve 800% to 1,000% ROI or profit margin. To them, the business textbook examples of 20-30% targets, often seen in the boardrooms of most companies, are child's play.

To see Cost is Actually to Reduce it

How can a company start a continuous cost-reduction movement? First, it will have to get everybody together to start this gold mine, called cost, 'in the company's backyard. Cost should be made the concern and responsibility of every employee. Everybody becomes not only a quality centre but cost centre as well. Every employee has both a quality responsibility and a cost responsibility.

To help them carry out this responsibility, information about costs should be made available to all employees. The companies make such costs visible to everybody so that they may attract attention and prompt action. In cost reduction, ignorance is not an excuse.

In many Japanese world-class companies, the costs of all parts and supplies are posted on the factory bulletin boards for everyone to see. The costs of every kind of product defect are also displayed. These include material costs and the cost of wasted labour and utilities consumed by such defects. Costs of non-tangible items may also be shown—cost per hour of machine downtime, electrical consumption per machine, overtime, etc. The management is less concerned with the leakage of such information to competitors through its employees than with preventing employees because of sheer ignorance of costs.

If a small part, say, a bolt, is accidentally dropped on the shop floor, no worker will bother to pick it up and return it to the tray. Somebody may even kick it. But replace that bolt with a Rs. 5/- coin, its true cost to the company, then somebody will immediately pick it up. Now, if every worker is made aware that each bolt costs the company Rs. 5/- then everybody will handle each bolt if it were Rs. 5/- coin. Beware of small expenses; a small leak can sink a big ship.

Thus companies achieve mega-profitability through relentless quality improvement and cost reduction, while achieving the ultimate in customer satisfaction. Profit to them is not a goal or a target; it is the natural consequence of management of putting the customer first, and managing everything else with complete freedom and open-mindedness.

In order to achieve full advantage: First set the price at which the customer will buy, then bring down your costs so you can make profits. By making our product in very large numbers, the cost would come down as volume climbed. With greater volumes, the cost of the system can be amortized over the greater number of units produced.

CRP projects are categorised into Value Engineering, Manufacturing Process Improvement, Business Process Improvement, Cost Reduction and Negotiation Savings Programme etc. This benefits both the employees and the organisation. Benefits to employees includes different work than routine, improved job satisfaction, opportunities to move towards higher incentives, increased self-confidence and spirit to outperform. The organisation benefits by enhancing cost competitive advantage, providing higher value for money to customers, increased productivity and quality. This truly works like the people power by the magic of motivation and a will to win.

14

Evaluation and Management of Criticism—A Healthy Trend

INTRODUCTION

Criticism may be defined as the process of inviting mature reflection, comments, remarks and declaration from others on certain activities being decided. In an organization, **the Management of Criticism is an act of balancing to evaluate the good and bad; to create an environment congenial to openness, mutual trust, confidence, cooperation and coordination.** The criticism is like an under-current in a stream. Its positive and negative aspects are equality important to ensure work together as a team in an organization to achieve their commitment to common goals and objectives. The constructive criticism is a positive aspect to obtain significant contribution in the planned targets. This must ensure enhancing the enthusiasm and morale of their employees; to motivate them for continuous improvement in performance, quality, productivity and cost reduction etc by optimum use of their zeal, wisdom, intelligence, talent, knowledge, skills, integrity, innovation, initiative, creativity, capabilities, expertise, trustworthiness, dedication, effectiveness and efficiency. The employees needs and ambitions be synchronized with the **total organizational goals** and objectives.

STRATEGY

The employees criticism is unpleasant and it should be dealt with sensitively particularly to correct their errors or faults:

- (i) People build up a tolerance for criticism, as body builds defenses towards climatic changes.
- (ii) Everyone including Managers prefers to be liked and the exception to it are rare.
- (iii) The too much criticism of a valuable employee may out-motivate him not to improve upon his work but to seek other employment.

BARRIERS TO EFFECTIVE CRITICISM

Most people put up the following barriers and try to lower them slowly but assuredly:

- (i) A superior has the power to rewards, so some subordinates may feel that they will receive negative rewards, if they voice their criticism.
- (ii) Criticism can be stopped for fear of hostility.
- (iii) Some subordinates may feel, they can be demoted or degraded when they criticise their superior, hence they will not criticise.
- (iv) Fear of counter criticism can also serve as a mental block.
- (v) Some people are not inclined to be different from others. Therefore, whatever others say, it is accepted without any amendment. There are others who may feel that they do not have much knowledge about a matter, hence they keep silent.

OBJECTIVE

The fear of criticism is a state of mind which becomes translated into worry. Whether the criticism is done in a pleasant manner or otherwise, you can use it constructively for your own purposes. There are valid reason to criticise an employee such as:

(i) To motivate or stimulate him for better performance.
(ii) To make him understand, how his efforts are being judged and where he stands.
(iii) To maintain the standards laid-down for all employees.
(iv) Point out errors but be objective in your criticism to attain certain results constructive and valid.
(v) To get to the root of the problem and aim the goal you set for the results.
(vi) To make it clear to your subordinate, what you expect in terms of the result?

POTENTIAL BENEFITS AND COSTS OF CRITICISM

Criticism is a mixed blessing and following are **the bright side of the coin:**

(i) Criticism helps all the parties involved to improve knowledge.
(ii) Criticism helps individual to learn and react to the actions of others.
(iii) Criticism is a no-cost source of research.
(iv) Criticism promotes a team spirit as well as broadmindedness/open-mindedness of the human resources of an organization.
(v) Criticism is a non-monetary tool of motivation.
(vi) Criticism helps in achieving organizational goals and objectives.
(vii) Criticism helps the realization of hidden mistakes to overcome various bottlenecks.

Despite its benefits, it renders the following costs, which are **the dark side of the coin:**

(i) Criticism paves the way to enmity and hostility between those who frame policies and those who implement them. The **gunine tragedies in the world are not conflicts between right and wrong but they**

are conflicts between rights.

(ii) Criticism may lead to industrial dispute. It creates an unpleasant, undisciplined atmosphere in an organization,

(iii) Criticism may result in unhealthy conflicts in an organization, undermining its human resources base.

(iv) Criticism could also kill the spirit of initiative.

(v) A superior may feel hurt or insulted when his subordinates pinpoint his shortcomings and tussles. There is a story that Badshah Akbar asked Birbal (one out of his Navaratnas Minister) to paint his portrait. Birbal completed it within a week. Badshah called his remaining eight Navaratnas and asked them to comment on it. Each one put a dot on the portrait, wherever he felt it was not good. Badshah asked Birbal to explain. Highly talented Birbal called for eight blank canvases for his colleagues and Badshah asked them to do the portrait. No one came forward to start this job. Badshah, with dropping eyes murmured, "Stupid Doters." The moral of the story is that it is easy to find faults in job done by others, but really difficult to do it yourself.

(vi) In business and industry, argument is an poor system of thinking since it is to do with win, lose, defence, attack and ego which are emotional things. As we normally see in a court of law, the plaintiff and the defendant will both present their cases to an independent judge. Both plaintiff and defendant will often represent interpretations radically different supported by evidence of a set of events. The judge decides which interpretation is correct and determines who wins out of the two.

ORGANISE MORE POSITIVE AND EFFECTIVE CRITICISM

Criticism can be made more positive on the following areas:

(i) Do not perceive criticism as something bad/a shortcoming. If you feel it is unworthy of you, turn a deaf ear to it. **What a blessing it would be if we could open and shut our ears as easily as we do our eyes.**

(ii) Give sometime for the dust to settle down when someone is rude in his criticism as, with time, its impact will be diluted.

(iii) If you are criticised unfairly, defend yourself and stand by your conviction.

(iv) Perceive criticism as a source of potential help in making-wise decisions.

(v) Do not arm the critic by counter attacking.

(vi) Do not raise your voice above the voice of critic. Let him go ahead and be mild and amicable with him.

Criticism is like the double-edged sword and can easily be made more effective as a potential business management tool by followings:

(i) Selecting, leading, and conducive spots where critics can come together and draw their views verbally, non-verbally, publicly or anonymously.

(ii) Perceive critics as a vital source to help, solve and implement solutions for the problems raised.

(iii) Explore the critic's views fully and freely, providing all sorts of ways in which critics can express their deliberations without hesitation.

PLANNING

Set priorities to succeed in long run. Therefore, manage to balance between work and personal activities. **If you don't take care of the person, you won't be able to take care of the work. Let your employees know that you value them first and their contribution to your work second. The following points are narrated for your reflection:**

(i) Never compromise where your goodwill and image is likely to be tarnished.

(ii) Keep patience and deal politely to minimize your differences with those in authority. But remember that your polite and lenient nature should never be misunderstood for weakness.

(iii) Discuss matter in a natural, straight and simple way since the misrepresentation will harm in long run rather than to bring you gain.

(iv) Deal and develop contacts in a logical and scientific way with the person who are known for best reputation and impartiality in their dealing.

(v) The dealing with strangers should be started carefully since the performance during dealing reveals their nature.

(vi) Do not desire to take revenge which may always disturb you.

(vii) Never make false promises.

(viii) Never advise your employees ten times a day. Advise very selectively so that they can work on their own.

(ix) Your conduct should be so fair, that people should never regret having dealt with you.

(x) News travel very fast in an organization because of human curiosity. Use it to send the required message but make sure that the massage is not distorted.

(xi) Make sure that the control mechanism is working according to expectations and informations are shared among all concerned.

STYLE AND SKILLS

Please remember, you are part of the system; and you cannot function and flourish in isolation. Your style and skills of criticism are critically important. The manner in which we talk is a part of our personality. Our style of speaking remains almost the same, since we have moderate control over it. The self-criticism is characteristic of a mature mind and essential for self development, the absence of which limits the potential for growth. You should continue to trust and use your intuition when appropriate. Don't over-rely on logic which sometimes leads to incorrect conclusion. **Please be selective in your choice of criticism:**

(i) Ensure the minimum emotional damage to either side and maximum positive results for both the parties. Do not insult anybody.

(ii) Ensure that the discussion does not punch or hurts, the ego or sentiments of an individual.

(iii) Do not form a premature impression about anyone until you have studied the situation properly.

(iv) The open dialogues even of conflict and difference of opinions are essential to encourage new ideas of creativity and innovation in the changing environment of organizational effectiveness. The discussion should be constructive to avoid confrontation.

(v) **Ensure to criticise the act, not the individual person.** This makes the discussion easier and more effective. The personal attack increases the defensiveness to the extent that the person may avoid to take care even of the valid points.

(vi) If malicious rumours are being spread against you, the patience always reveals the truth. Therefore, reply only at a time favourable to you in such circumstances.

(vii) Resolve dispute quickly with those whom you consider bad, even if you have to make some sacrifice. Never be *disheartened* and if you cannot render justice sometimes in your decision then end the dispute without further complications.

(viii) It is easier for someone to change his behaviour than to change his basic nature. So you focus on the facts (not the man) to obtain realistic results.

(ix) Select time to criticise in private which ensures minimum interruptions and makes the discussion effective.

(x) Your criticism becomes more convincing when it is based on facts and then you are in a better position to find remedy with the errant employee. Make your comments only when you are sure of the facts.

(xi) **Criticise someone at the right place and right time for justified complaints** through a proper channel and do not hold any personal grudge towards anyone.

(xii) Be generous in praising good work. Always praise loudly but blame softly. Praise to make an individual know about his image in your mind which is the good criticism sound as a reward.

(xiii) **Avoid angry confrontations** which is a harmful emotion. The outburst of bad temper for a moment can create a serious consequence in solving the problem and make the stressful situation worse. The consequences of anger is best illustrated in the Bhagawad Gita, Chapter 2, Text 63 as under:

क्रोधाद्भवति सम्मोहः सम्मोहात्स्मृतिविभ्रमः।
स्मृतिभ्रंशाद् बुद्धिनाशो बुद्धिनाशात्प्रणश्यति।।

From anger, arises complete false belief and the complete false belief results confusion of memory. The confusion of memory results loss of intelligence and the consequences of loss of intelligence results in extremely destroyed.

फिर क्रोध से है मोह, सुधि को मोह करता भ्रष्ट है।
यह सुधि गए फिर बुद्धि-विनशे, बुद्धि-विनशे नष्ट है।।

A cool disposition will always pay you dividend.

(xiv) Better do not be aggressive to win at all costs. **Do not talk when you lose your temper, since there is chance for slip of your tongue which exists only one in between thirty two teeth.** Keeping quiet gives you time to cool down and decide positively. This facilitates you to talk about feelings openly in a non-hostile and congenial manner.

(xv) Establish your confidence in individual employee and help him when it is desired. **Do not let ego come in your way.** If your subordinate does his job, then you have done yours. He is not your competitor but he is your stepping stone. You should have maturity to accept a competent subordinate.

THINK BEFORE YOU CRITICISE

We make friends who speak good about us, since we all like to earn praise, reward and recognition. When anyone criticize us, we become defensive in our explanation and try to give evidence to prove ourselves correct; irrespective of the actual facts. While criticising others, it is equally important to search our own heart to improve upon the short-comings of ourselves effectively. Remember! when you raise a finger on anyone, there are three fingers on you. When you are good to others, you are best to yourself.

I would like to quote here a example from Ramayana in which Rama forgive Kaikai and forget. Rama search his own heart and realised his shortcomings that it would have been fair on his part to wait for Raj Tilak until his brothers had come to join the ceremony. The moral of this example is that you should retain those thoughts in your memory, which give you happiness and discard those thoughts, which give you heartburns. The decent and cultured people are noble, successful and happy since they forgive liberally to their enemies and forget. This is a win win game where many enemies become true friend.

There is a another story often quoted by Osho Rajnish. A poor holy person was interested in discovering God. So, one day, he went to the nearby church and knocked the door. The priest opened the door but advised him to do some prayer and other purification process before he could be allowed in the church. He did meditations and prayers again for a year and was on way to the church. He met a person while going to the church. This was infact God himself who informed him that since church has been build, he is trying to enter but he has not been allowed. How he expects to enter? The God requested him to forget about it.

SHARED VALUE

Good criticism energize. Bad criticism enervate. Good criticism is an art of making problem so interesting and their solutions so constructive, that everyone wants to deal with them to achieve the object as per expectation. Develop a common value system and expertise in making critical decisions.

RECOGNITION AND REWARD

The minds are conquered by love and high mindedness and not by force. Happiness is never perfect unless it is shared. Therefore, the praise for good work is really necessary. When someone does an excellent work, the reward is what they get personally and the recognition is what they get publicly. You will find that your most productive employees are the ones, who are most marketable and they are most likely to leave your organization. Therefore, pay for performance specially for long term gain. Don't forget those opportunities to praise and complement others. Remember to acknowledge good performance and excellent results.

15

Learning Culture and Human Resource Development— Bringing into Talents

"If you want to be prosperous for a year, grow grains. If you want to be prosperous for 10 year, grow trees. If you want to be prosperous for a lifetime, grow people."

—*An Ancient Proverb*

PREAMBLE

A Learning Organisation is one in which employees at all levels, individually and collectively; increases continually their capacity, skills, efficiency and effectiveness to produce excellent results and performance. Employees quickly learn to flourish new ideas to improve their personal skills, qualities, creativity, values, growth, performance and bring in novel solutions to problems leading to innovation in their work.

Many industries have said for a long time that **"Our employees are our best assets"**. But they need to maximize the potential of their talented human resources for **VALUE ADDITION.** The policy either threaten your employees with dire consequences or provide them carrot in terms of monitory awards to improve the over-all results which is not a long lasting correct solution. Therefore, we need to maximize their individual competence by encouraging non-stop learning culture in organization.

Learning while earning is a noble profession. Training should be continued from recruitment to retirement. Continuous upgradation of knowledge and skill is a necessity in today's fast changing environment. Technologies are constantly changing. No one on the executive path can afford the luxury of not upgrading himself. Self -development is a key to executive success. The enthusiasm to develop yourself is a key to executive success. The enthusiasm to develop yourself should not cloud the need for a goal; a direction and a plan. Work out own self-development plans and then implement them.

LEARNING CULTURE

The learning culture is where people are interested in acquiring information, knowledge, skill, insight and foresight. These aspects of learning are important and unless these aspects are covered, there is no Human Resource Development. There are three areas in which a person may develop. The first is **"Contribution Value."** Everybody sitting in his workplace, is contributing to the organisation. We need to learn how to improve this contribution. The input of additional information about technology and techniques upgradation can improve the contribution value and we can see people improving their contribution value steadily. But that is only one part of development. The second part of development is in the field of **"Transfer Value."** Take a person contributing to his specific job in a specific department. Suppose he goes to another function or to another department or to another company, how well would he perform? That depends on three things: The first is the extent of his **"learning"**, second is the widening **of his "horizons"** and third is his **ability to "project an image".**

THE LEARNING PROCESS

Let us look at "learning." The best way to understand learning is to see a small child. A child at the age of 2-3 months gets up in the morning and starts talking, i.e. makes noises. Then realizes that the stupid adults around him can't understand him. Why? Because human being is the only creation that requires a language -to communicate. All other animals seem to communicate just by making noises. So a child decides that it must acquire vocabulary the **"information"**. As soon as he becomes around 6 months old, he starts asking questions: What is this- orange, What is the colour-Yellow. What is that colour-Green. When it is asking all these questions, it is trying to acquire vocabulary. This is the first stage of learning i.e. information.

Contribution Value

After sometime, the child starts relating **information** and then it becomes **"knowledge"**. For example, it realizes that water has to be stored in a container, it can't be stored by itself. That is knowledge; when the child applies the knowledge, it becomes **"skill"**. You ask a two year old child to bring water. It puts water in a glass and brings the filled glass. That is skill. If we look at ourselves, all of us have acquired lot of skills which are vital for our **"contribution value"**.

Transfer Value

The next stage of learning is **"insight"**. Many people have knowledge and skill, but they don't have insight. For example, I asked one lady who was making some curry. She boils water, adds some ingredients at one point of time, spices at another point of time, chilies at third point, salt at another point and so on. I ask her "Why do you add different items at different time? Why not get everything together, put in a pressure cooker and cook. It will save your time-and it will save energy." What does she say? "We always do it this way. Please don't bother me." She has skill. She makes very good curries. But she doesn't have insight. The other day, I asked another lady the same question. She said, "Look here- If we add salt right at the beginning, the boiling point of water would go up and consequently the ingredients may get overcooked. If we add spices right at the beginning, some of them are volatile. When you sit down to eat the curry, there might be no flavour left." This lady has not only the skill, but also the insight.

Very few managers acquire insight. When you ask a manager, "Why are you doing so in this way," what is his response? "That is our procedure. We always do it that way. It is according to the Instructions Manual of this company." This means, the person does not know why he is doing it.

Out of those who know why, very few people are able to project themselves to ask: "Whatever we are doing today, how far is it valid for the future?" This shows **"foresight"**, i.e. the ability to project and see the future. Out of total who have skills, only less than 1% have the foresight to look at things and understand their role for the future.

Out of those who have foresight, a few use this foresight for the benefit of the community-not for their personal benefit. This is "wisdom". As we can see, there are six stages of learning (i) information, (ii) knowledge, (iii) skill, (iv) insight, (v) foresight, and (vi) wisdom. Most people acquire upto skill stage. If you desire to acquire transfer value, then at least the insight and foresight are required. Sanskrit is a very rich language. In Sanskrit, each type of teacher is given a different designation as under:

Gives	*Designation*
Information	Adhyapaka
Knowledge	Upadhyaya
Skill	Acharya
Insight	Pandit
Foresight	Drishta
Wisdom	Guru

As Kabir said "Guru Gobind dou Khade, kake lago paay,

balihari Guru Apane, Gobind diyo batay" (If Guru and God are both standing, first salute the Guru. Guru is even greater than the God because you understand what is God, only if you have Guru.)

Guru should not be greedy like Guru Daronacharya in Mahabharat. The story to learn from Daronacharya and Eklavya is illustrated below:

Raj Guru Daronacharya was the great teacher in Mahabharat. He only taught the princes but refused to Eklavya and Karana who were from backward class.

Eklavya make an earthen statue of Daronacharya and started practising archery before him. Eklavya being self-motivated and self-inspired started practicing for long hours and achieved perfection in archery. Once Daronacharya was meditating in his ashram when a barking dog created hue and cry in the surroundings. Instantly, the barking stopped. Curiously Daronacharya came out of the ashram and he saw the dog with arrows in his open mouth! He enquired who did it!! Eklavya appeared in front of the great guru in all modesty.

Daronacharya: "Who gave you this education?"

Eklavya: "Daronacharyaji."

Daronacharya: "I am Daronacharya, what about my Guru Dakshina?"

Eklavya: "I will be honoured to do according to your orders."

Daronacharya: "Give me your right hand thumb."

Eklavya did it immediately in respect of his Guru.

For transfer value, you need to acquire at least insight and foresight-and this is an important aspect of learner. With the foresight, people can widen their horizons. The projecting image- as long as you are doing a job, everybody in the company knows how well you are doing it. But when you are thinking of going to another job, people wonder: "Can you do some other function, work effectively in some other department, other location or even another company?" Then your image counts. Acquiring this image is a very important aspect in transfer value.

Acquiring the projecting image does not mean that people will leave the organization. I would like to give a very simple example: Let each of us look at his mother, wife and daughter. We can see how the transfer value has changed in these three generations. In the case of your mother, probably she had no transfer value inspite of high contribution value. If your father did not respect her high contribution value, then she had no choice but to bear it. As you can see, your wife has much better transfer value. She has acquired some learning not merely in terms of education or book-learning, but also learning about the world. Your mother may still require an escort to travel. Your wife can travel on her own. This is the transfer value she has acquired through learning and widening her horizons. When it comes to your daughter, she will prefer to travel on her own. This is because of a further improvement in the transfer value.

Thus, increased transfer value does not mean a rapid turnover. It only increases the possibility of turnover. In every organization, we find a few people sitting in some corner and collectively cursing the organization and their fate. After all, no organization can keep everybody satisfied. Somebody or the other is affected adversely by some decisions of the company. If he has no transfer value, all he can do is to sit down and curse. The great advantage of transfer value is that people will think of a change rather than sit in the organization and curse. They will go out, find their avenues and opportunities.

The transfer value also helps people to think about delegation. As long as a person believes that there is only one chair he has in this world from which he can contribute and if he gets out of this chair, there is nothing he can do, he is unlikely to delegate-inspite of all the sermons we give him. Where a person feels: "I am doing the present job for five years- may be that I shall do it for another one or two years more. Then I must do something else." If this is the attitude, then obviously the person is likely to develop subordinates and is likely to delegate. Thus, HRD for the individual himself as well as for his subordinates depends a lot on how much transfer value is acquired. So this transfer value is a very important aspect of human resource development. When one acquires wisdom and knowledge, then he sparks like a diamond. He can't remain in dark.

Leisure Value

The next situation is when a person stops working. After all, however senior a person is, however hard working, he is, there will be some evening when there will be a gathering of people where he gets a bouquet of flowers, a wrist watch' with words like "live happily hereafter". But ultimately: "Get out and don't come again." That is the end of work. What does he do the next day?

A person has to spend his time even after retirement, when he has nothing to do. We learn what to do on the job but we don't know what to do when the job is no more! This is where learning for the Leisure Value becomes relevant. After all, we are supposed to "enjoy" leisure. People work for 35 to 40 years of their life. Thereafter, they are supposed to retire and enjoy the retired life. But how many do so? Most of the people I meet after retirement are miserable. Just the other day, I was attending a farewell function of a General Manager who was retiring. He started his address with the words. 'My funeral procession has started—and I don't know how long it will be'! If people are not prepared, the leisure is not an opportunity, it is a calamity. If people prepare themselves with the leisure value, i.e. with hobbies, they are able to deal with the time after retirement and that will make the retirement an opportunity and not a calamity.

WAYS TO IMPROVE LEARNING CULTURE

There is a story of Badshah Akbar and his minister Birbal. Once Badshah got angry with Birbal and said, he should be executed. Birbal was worried and tried to get pardon in many ways. But Badshah was firm—no pardon! So Birbal called a trust worthy friend and said, "Go to the

Badshah and make a proposal." The friend said, "What kind of proposal can you make to Badshah?" Birbal said, "Tell Badshah, I shall train his favourable horse to fly in twelve months—and he should give me pardon." The friend said, "May be, the Badshah will accept this proposal, but how can you make such a proposal?" Birbal said, "What do I lose? In the next twelve months, the Badshah may die—good chance of getting pardon from the successor! Or in the next twelve months, the horse may die—I get another horse and another twelve months. Or in the next twelve months, I may die—in which case I need no pardon. Or who knows may be in the next twelve months, the horse may learn to fly! There is always a chance." So many times, training seminars are organised with the hope that the participants may learn.

Learning never stops and with conscious efforts, the experience can be made more rewarding. Sending people to learning courses has an important contribution to make. People learn at different speeds and different ways. They need opportunities to think, experiment, test and reflect on their experience. People spend several hundred hours each year in learning efforts outside the schools and training programmes, i.e. they are learning on their own from people around themselves. The people who help them learn are not teachers and trainers but co-workers, bosses and employees.

The steps to improve your ability to maximise learning at the work place are given below:

Know Your Employees

Knowing your employee gives clues to what they are learning and their need to learn. To know your people, keep the following points in mind.

(i) Be familiar with their background and current concerns.
(ii) Problems which individual is facing in job or personal life.
(iii) Preferred manner of learning of individual.
(iv) Barriers which are hindering the learning.

(v) What individual did that, enabled them to learn successfully in the past.

(vi) Correlation between individual career plan and what you want them to learn.

Provide a Learning Environment

Learning is facilitated by a low stress environment, a state of relaxed alertness and a sense of confidence in one's capacity. Kill grimness with laughter. Maintain an atmosphere of informality. Encourage high spirits. Get rid of sadness that spread gloom.

Promote Learning by Self Discovery

Knowledge self-discovered is stored in the deepest part of the mind and remains for the longest in the memory. The important aspects to promote learning by self discovery are as under:

(i) Plan, design and place the sequence of jobs to suit the individual's knowledge and ability.

(ii) Make all the information required for doing the job readily available.

(iii) Allow them to find out things for themselves.

(iv) Let the trainer merely act as a guide.

I would like to quote an allegory. Once a person close to Badshaha Akbar was requested by the villagers to go to Badshaha for some help for the village. When he approached Badshaha, Badshaha was praying God and asking God for more wealth and extension for his empire. This person heard Badshaha prayers and returned back with remark that 'he himself is a beggar, how can a beggar give relief out of pity to the poor?'

Use Mistakes to Train Your Employee

People commit mistakes and learn from them. If you live in fear, you will never take risks and gain the learning. You will not admit your mistakes, if you are likely to be blamed.

Helping people to learn from mistakes involves:

(i) Action: mistake is seen as caused by inadequate training or supervision, or the use of wrong materials. The person points it out and gets it rectified.

(ii) Communication: i.e. saying something which help to eliminate that type of error in future.

There is a story regarding Sharpen your axe which is given below:

> Once upon a time, a very strong woodcutter asked for a job to a timber merchant, and he got it. The pay was really good and so were the working conditions. For that reason, the woodcutter was determined to do his best. His boss gave him an axe and showed him the area where he was supposed to work. The first day, the woodcutter brought 16 trees. "Congratulations," the boss said. "Carry on that way!" Very motivated with the boss's words, the woodcutter tried harder the next day, but he could bring only 12 trees. The third day he tried even harder, but could bring 8 trees only. Day after day he was bringing less and less trees. "I must be losing my strength", the woodcutter thought. He went to the boss and apologized, saying that he could not understand what was going on wrong.

"When was the last time you sharpened your axe?" The boss asked. Woodcutter replied, "Sharpen? I had no time to sharpen my axe. I have been very busy trying to cut more trees for you."

Our lives are like that. We sometimes get so busy that we don't take time to "sharpen the axe". Why is that? Could it be that we have forgotten how to stay sharp?

There's nothing wrong with activity and hard work. We are so busy that we neglect the truly important things in life, like taking time to read, to exercise, to care etc. We all need time to relax, to think and meditate, to learn and grow. If we don't take time to "sharpen our axe", then we will all become dull and lose our effectiveness.

So start today, think about the ways by which you could do your job more effectively and add a lot of value to it. Remember any thing that is stagnated would get rotten, would smell badly—be it air or water or even a professional.

"Iron rusts from disuse,
Stagnant water loses its purity,
and in cold weather becomes frozen,
even so does inaction sap the vigor of the mind."

—Leonardo De Vinci

Provide free access to your employee to contact the person with know-how

Learning involves the person with intellect, emotions, values, perceptions and the experience. Most people who want to learn will choose a friendly human being. Make sure that learners have the access to people who have know-how. There is an ancient saying—

> "Give your son Rs. 1000/- and he will spent for a day. Better, teach him how to earn Rs. 1000/- per day and he will spent forever."

Make Employees Believe that they are Doing Well

Learning proceeds most effectively when the learner is motivated. The prime factor is the self-perception among motivated subjects that they are doing well. Success apparently leads to higher motivation to make things better.

Let Employees have Access to Modern Learning Methods

The success of the advanced education clearly indicate three things.

(i) People are thirsty for knowledge.
(ii) People are prepared to learn in their spare time.
(iii) People are attracted to open and flexible learning methods.

Therefore, to help people learn in their spare time, introduce them to modern learning methods like distance learning, action learning and computer based training.

Encourage them to pursue their personal development through choosing within their own capability limits, the methods, pace and times in which they can learn and reward them for the mastery of new skills.

The concept of knowledge is like the story of THE HERMIT AND THE CHAIN SAW. One day an old Hermit came to buy a saw at the local hardware store. "I am building for myself a new long home," the Hermit said to the young sales clerk, "I need the best saw you got—and price is not an object." The young sales clerk disappeared into the warehouse for a moment and returned with a gleaming new chain saw. "This is the best saw on the market," and sales clerk said confidently. "It will cut through trees like a knife through butter. I guarantee, it will cut a months worth of lumber in a day—or I will personally refund your money from my paycheck!" The excited Hermit paid the clerk and taken his gleaming new chain saw.

Exactly one month later the young clerk was busy stocking shelves, when he heard the Hermit's voice crack through the air like whip. "Hey, I have come to return this saw and get my money back, like you promised." The clerk see the old Hermit looked like he had not slept in weeks and worked hard. "What happened to you?" the clerk stammered. "You look terrible!.

The old Hermit summoned all his strength and lifted his chain saw on to the counter, grumbling, "It is this deadburn saw you sold me. You said it had cut a month's worth of lumber in a day. Well, I have been using this contraption for 30 days now and I am unable to cut a day's worth of lumber in a month. I want my money back!" The clerk apologised and said, "Sure, a deal is a deal. Just let me have a look at this saw for you. May be, I can figure out what's wrong." The clerk gave the pull rope a quick yank and the chainsaw exploded into a roar. The Hermit jumped back from the counter like he had been shot, Shouting over the roaring saw, "What's that sound?" Can you imagine trying to cut down a tree with a chain saw that was not even turned on? No wonder, the Hermit looked beat up and worn out. The chain saw is obviously a great tool and you know exactly the difference, If you have ever tried to cut up a big tree limb using a hand saw.

The irony of the story is the Hermit had in his hand a powerful tool but he just did not know how to use it. In other words, his failure did not result from a lack of talent or effort. His failure resulted from a lack of knowledge.

CONCLUSION

In conclusion, let me review the basic concepts of human resource development. Most of the organisation, use Human Resource Development exclusively as training in which a real love for human being is not there and they cannot churn to get gems out of human resources. Due to this, the people now feel that the operation has been successful but the patient died. In fact, Human Resource Development is not training, it is learning. The responsibility for learning is on the training department which makes the facilities available, on the immediate boss who can give counselling to the subordinate, and on the individual who is going to develop.

People learn contribution value and transfer value in their professional life. Ultimately, there is no dispute that there is life after retirement-and for many people, that life is almost half their working life. If they are not prepared for that life, then they will have long years of misery. To avoid this situation, learning is required for the "Leisure Value." In Japan, they feel that anybody is fit to be a manager only if he has two abilities: Firstly, he is able to get consensus with his subordinates on any problem that they are facing and secondly, if he can train his subordinates in what he knows. This is the boss's role in Human Resource Development. The boss has to take responsibility to see that his subordinates get their Contribution Value, Transfer Value and Leisure Value. Ultimately, we shall learn not only in the area of information, knowledge and skills, but also in the area of insight, and foresight-may be some of us may get even wisdom, which is the foundation of all successful livings.

The future belongs to the free trade and competitive market. The success of the entrepreneur will depend on his ability to evolve a competitive edge in his business. New opportunities will depend on innovativeness and fast paced responses to take advantage of its inherent strengths and flexibility of operations. Achieving global competitiveness requires excellent performance on multiple dimension like cost, quality, delivery and flexibility.

The lowering of tariff, recessionary trends, entry of multinationals and specially marketing of products and its services have posed major challenges. The liberalization and globalization has changed the scenario to look forward for competition at global market. It is not enough, to just manage an organisation effectively for achieving corporate excellence. Therefore, the success of organisations depends upon the strength of its human resources which has been identified as the core of the whole system. It is the art of inspiring the human resources which ultimately bring to reality, the dream and vision of the leader for optimum utilisation of time and all available resources. The art to enhance creativity and vision for persuing excellence, managing change, accomodating diversity and resolving conflicts is essential for increasing performance and capacity by collective wisdom in decision making process.

Excellence in organisation results from the way in which management harmonize their valuable human resource. The style of getting best out of people varies from one company to another. The today's mounting uncertainty and radical change give way to an enlightened approach that taps the energies of employees — both individually and in teams. Consequently, if organisation wants to prosper, it is of paramount importance to attract, retain and get the best from talented and high-performing individuals. In order to play a winning game, we must select winners for our team who have the right temperament for job assigned to them.

Human capital is the combined experiences, knowledge,

know-how, skills, ideas, creativity and inventions of a Company's employees, providing the cutting edge towards sustainable competitive advantage and creation of value for the organisation.

The present competent forces make it eminent that we must obtain organisational excellence. This can happen through the way the organisation get things done and how they treat their people to achieve results that enrich the organisational value to the customers, investors and employees. Growth is life and do not allow obstacles to stand in the way of success.

When you dare to think beyond creating business excellence and wealth creation, the companies need to do radically different things to stay far ahead than their competitors. There is a huge amount of untapped human innovative potential within the organisation that often remains largely idle and we are not able to translate their ideas into business reality. We seek to harness the huge wealth creation potential that exists within the organisation, by getting people to change their mindset to use their power and potential for the over-all good of the organisation. The personal growth, challenge and innovation are the motivation factors for individuals to adopt quickly new concepts and technologies.

Wealth creation will occur only when the organisation creates a culture of business innovation across all levels and in each sphere to enable employees to deliver their best potential. Further insights for getting value out of break-through technology and vision in succeeding against all odds are to be used in areas like development of value-added products, continuous improvement in the quality of products, drive to constant improvement of process, exploration of avenues for continuous cost reduction and development of new market segment. This can be achieved by increasing employees contribution by enhancing their commitment to the organisation and use their abilities to deliver the best results.

We need to create winning organisation which consists

capabilities like speed, responsiveness, quick action, learning capacity and employees competence. The successful organisation needs to develop qualities like: (i) quickly form strategy into action, (ii) process strategy intelligently and efficiently, (iii) Maximise employees contribution and commitment and (iv) create the condition for free flow of change etc. Thus efficiency can be improved of each process that can be done better, faster and cheaper. The key success factors for change are: (i) Who is responsible for leading change? (ii) Create a shared need as why to do it? (iii) shaping vision, (iv) Mobilising commitment and involvement; (v) Modifying the existing system, (vi) Monitoring progress, (vii) Get started and completed. The love to the organisation is the glue that holds the individuals and organisation together and binds them through the process of commitment.

Remember , to look at things from the other persons perspective, offer genuine appreciation, harness the power of enthusiasm and respect the dignity of others. For workforce and management it is true that:

"Coming together is the beginning,
Keeping together is the progress,
Working together is the success,
United together is the prosperity."

16

Personnel Handling—A Healing Touch

Motivation is what that makes people to deliver the desired results. Absence of motivation causes frustration, which makes a man submissive or aggressive. While working, if one gets happiness, there will be an urge for attaining perfection.

Neither money and power nor the threat is the essence of motivation. The essence of motivation, then, is to trust a man and entrust him with work for which he is most suitable. Make him believe that you have faith and confidence in him. This approach generally gives very good results.

STEPS TO KEEP AN EMPLOYEE DEVELOPED AND SATISFIED

Fault finding, especially in front of others and tight supervision provoke negative reactions. If a man makes a mistake, it is better that he is called aside privately and told about the best way to have done the job. Though he may try to justify his actions, he will not repeat the mistake.

Man basically aspires to continuously rise in life. But, like a machine, man needs maintenance and it is in the interest of the company that steps should be taken to appreciate his value. A leader should take the following steps to keep his men developed:

- Your men should not work as individuals, but should work as a team.
- Work yourself first, with speed otherwise your team members will be sluggish.
- To your staff —

  (i) Give responsibility.
  (ii) Delegate power.
  (iii) Give freedom of operation.
  (iv) Give guidance.

- Make them aware that time and cost overruns must be avoided.
- Make them feel that you have confidence in them.
- Praise them in public, but if need be, reprimand them in private.
- Extend support to a man at his workplace. Try to solve his personal problems, if needed.
- Review the workload and procedures; try to simplify them as far as possible.
- Be transparent with your staff, encourage discussions, accept constructive criticism and good suggestions.
- Ensure that your objective is clearly understood by your team members.
- Make sure of the exact role you expect your men to play.
- Provide training to update their knowledge.
- Keep a close watch on people who flatter you.
- Be polite and natural.
- Be fair and firm.
- People are important. Don't prick your subordinate's self-esteem.
- Put a man on the job where he fits best.
- Mistakes will be made. They can be minimised by proper monitoring and guidance. Don't look for faults, but find remedies.

CORRECT ERRING EMPLOYEES BY COUNSELLING

No two employees will be identical. There are good employees as well as bad employees. A problem guy is one who uses his emotions to destroy others or the organisation. You cannot eliminate him, but you have to make good use of him.

Here, counselling plays an important part. Counselling does not mean giving spiritual advise. It means sharing another's pain and emotions to enable him to release his tension and make him feel part of the organisation.

The following approach may be adopted for counselling:

- Prepare yourself for counselling. Be aware that you have to converse freely with the person about problems and what you can do to improve his performance.
- Talk to him in a friendly tone. Clarify the objective of the meeting. Tell him that he has been called not for apportioning blame, but to work out a solution jointly.
- Tell him, that the meeting will be kept confidential.
- Listen to the man patiently. Don't interrupt him, but, from time to time, ask for small clarifications to show that you are attentive and responding.
- Collect all the data you need from his statements, and identify the problem.
- Tell him that organisation needs him.
- Explain what was wrong. Ask him whether he has any suggestion to improve the situation.
- Tell him that you want him to be successful and happy. Suggest ways of overcoming the problem without criticising him.
- Therefore, formulate an 'action plan' in consultation with him.
- After some time, get regular feedback from the group-in-charge about the man's performance. In most of the cases, you will find an improvement. Then, put him on the back for his better performance.

An organisation consists of two wings—employees and management. Both these sides must, contribute positively for the growth of the organisation.

INDUSTRIAL RELATIONS

A good manager should tune his mind to the following facts of lives:

- The law provides more than adequate support to the employees as they are considered the weaker section.
- The employer want to earn more money whereas employees need more money. Hence, there is nothing wrong if the employees demand more money.
- Employees may be individually good, but collectively, they often display mob behaviour.
- Whenever there is a battle between the management and employees, politicians and other negative forces will be waiting to use the disagreement to their best advantage.

With these realities in mind, a manager should deal with the situation in view of the aspirations of all sections of the organisation. His basic aim should be to maintain good and peaceful industrial relations while seeing that his organisation is not harmed.

DISCIPLINE IN INDUSTRY

An employer hires a best person out of several applicants, and offers him wages with the expectation that the employee will work faithfully and peacefully.

It is obligatory for an employee to carry out his assigned duties as per the service conditions. If he does not do his job, or shows disobedience or insubordination, he runs the risk of losing his job.

If an employee wants to change his service conditions, he has to ask the employer for his consideration. An employee has no right to refuse work if his demands are not fulfilled.

The employer expect decent conduct from the employees and reasonable returns in exchange of the wages taken by them.

Unless otherwise specified in the service rules, an employee is expected to do, in addition to his normal duties, incidental duties, related duties, ancillary duties, etc., which are expected by from one of his post, and not inferior.

For example, a messenger boy, in addition to moving papers, is also expected to make tea, bring refreshments, maintain files, etc. Punctuality in attendance, remaining at the work site, not going out of station without permission, are some valid expectations from employees.

Repeated incompetence and negligence in work despite counselling and opportunities for improvement, is punishable. Misconduct due to lack of integrity is to be dealt with severely.

Remember, it would be impossible to maintain discipline unless you, yourself, and other managers are a disciplined. While taking any disciplinary action, always consult your superiors and act through the Office of Manager (Industrial Relations).

WHY A MANAGER FAILS

Managers fail to motivate others and cannot mobilise the resources of an organisation when they:

- Rarely go to the shopfloor or work site, but remain busy doing paper work.
- They busy themselves in finding ways and means to improve their personal lives.
- They find innovative ways of punishing an offender instead of counselling him or setting an example themselves.
- They are glued to their boss for personal gain.
- They do not have clear objectives.
- They place the rule before the man.

A GLOWING CHARCOAL CAN IGNITE ANOTHER. A manager busy in activities described above, finds it difficult to lead his team. He has to face truly embarrassing questions from the employees when he addresses them about their organisational goals.

A manager must ensure that involvement of each employee is provided with the right avenues and encouragements to contribute their best to the organisation. The practice of participative management should be adopted to achieve excellence and sustain it. People cannot be truly motivated by anyone else except their working atmosphere which must foster self-motivation. People with self-motivation can drive themselves even to the level of par-excellence.

17

The Management and the Manager —A Combination

PREAMBLE

The management is a profession and the Manager is a professional, who practice it. The Organisation must have the Manager in order to function. The Manager has a client i.e., the enterprise. He is bound to sacrifice his own interests to safeguard the interest of his enterprise.

The Management is concerned with monitoring, facilitating and directing the accomplishment of organisational objectives, which depends mainly on skillful handling of the problems and opportunities.

THE QUALITIES OF MANAGER

(i) The Manager do not make decisions by opinions nor according to his preferences. They manage the right diagnosis through the force of facts and not through the force of personality.

(ii) The job of Manager is not to like or dislike certain employees and criticise subordinates in public but to have the trait to put their strengths to work together.

(iii) The 'performance' of Manager is setting an example which requires the integrity.

(iv) The Manager has talent for getting right things done.

The dissent, even conflict, is necessary for better understanding to avoid wrong decisions.

(v) The rank of Manager does not confer privilege or power but it imposes responsibility.

(vi) THE EFFECTIVE MANAGER .....

(a) Possess human skills like ability to understand, communicate clearly and capability to work with others.

(b) Possess conceptional skill—understanding, ability to organise, make predictions and solve problems.

(c) Has influence to get ideas and recommendations accepted by superiors.

(d) Uses scientific approaches but also trusts an intuitive sense.

(e) Perceives as Manager as well as a team member.

MANAGERIAL RESPONSIBILITIES

Whenever two or more people engage in a work activity together, there exist a need for coordination and direction. The Manager performs four main responsibilities effectively i.e., planning, organising, directing and controlling:

Planning

(a) Converting general plans and objectives into daily activity and make assignments suited to employees capability.

(b) Give explicit instructions on what is expected in the assignment.

(c) The work load according to employees capacity.

(d) Think ahead and be receptive to change.

Organising

The resources for performing the work involves personnel and facilities as well as coordinating the efforts of people:

(a) Make certain the facilities, equipment and supplies

are setup and ready for use.

(b) Build team-work and coordinate their activities.

(c) Improve methods and procedures.

Directing

Appropriate work assignments through delegation, instruction and coaching the employees to discharge their responsibilities correctly:

(a) Build confidence by providing clear and accurate expectations of your employees activities.

(b) Keep open communication with correlated departments.

(c) Devote time and attention to employees orientation and form relationships that leads to positive and open interactions.

Controlling

Making certain that performance meets the necessary standards and monitoring the flow and output of work:

(a) Controlling in advance is much better than disciplinary action after the fact.

(b) Feedback and follow-up is necessary for assessing progress, direction and consequences of performance.

(c) Develop positive attitude and work habit to build mental discipline to avoid the disciplinary action.

18

An Efficient and Effective Manager—The Basic Pillar

In order to ensure successful running of any organization, the efficient and effective Management of ten M's viz, (i) Men; (ii) Money; (ii) Material; (iv) Machines; (v) Methods; (vi) Market; (vii) Minute; (viii) Measurement; (ix) Motivation; and (x) Motto are most essential inputs.

ATTRIBUTES OF MANAGER

The following are the qualities required in a Manager:

(i) He has to be committed to his job.
(ii) He has to have loyalty towards the organization, he is working for.
(iii) He must have leadership qualities.
(iv) He must inspire his people to work hard.
(v) He should understand the problems of the workers and try to redress them.
(vi) In brief, he has to be a go-getter.

TIPS FOR MANAGERS

In view of the vital role that a Manager plays, some of the tips are given below:

(i) Identify your strength.
(ii) Be positive in your thoughts about yourself.
(iii) Review your past successes.
(iv) Have a vision.
(v) Turn the vision into a well defined, attainable objective.
(vi) Visualize the objective.
(vii) Act to achieve the objective.
(viii) Preserve towards the objective.
(ix) Keep appreciating the achievements.

HOW TO GET OPTIMUM RESULTS

In order to deliver optimum output, the management and the staff should have (i) shared goal ; (ii) work culture; (iii) continuous learning; (iv) positive effort and (v) Shared information.

MANAGER'S SUCCESS FORMULA

We are at the new millennium and moving towards the globalisation. This has brought in the need: (i) for global perspective (ii) global competence and (iii) to be equipped to cater for consumers unknown to them. Information Technology (IT) is making rapid strides and holds the key to future.

Manager's success has to cover:

IT orientation, Global—perspective, Adaptability to new structures, Sensitivity to different cultures, Language skills, Industry foresight, High task orientation, Self reliance, Innovation and Strategic awareness.

TIME—ESSENCE OF CONTRACT

'Time is the essence of contract'. Managers, by advancing planning, monitoring and corrective action, should see that delay does not happen.

HOW TO ASSESS PERSONALITY

All human beings are unique in their own sense and have been endowed with a mixed qualities. Curiosity, hard work, perseverance, determination, adaptability, honesty, humility, sensitivity, responsible attitude and an open mind are some of the time-tested strong points.

But a strong point of personality is of no use till it is actually put to some use. One should assess oneself honestly. Let his success and satisfaction be his guide.

STEPS TO HAPPINESS

The output of a person depends on whether he is happy or not. Here are steps pertaining to happiness:

(i) Live in the present.
(ii) Take control of your time. While you may set big goals, break them into daily and achieve them.
(iii) Accentuate the positive and take steps to keep negative emotions in check.
(iv) Don't be idle. Get involved in something that utilises your skills.

THE DRIVE OF ENTHUSIASM

"Nothing succeeds like success." One cannot achieve much unless he is prepared to take risks. People who are ready to take risks should be prepared to face failures. It is okay to fail as long as one did it with speed, learnt a lesson and moved on. Executing a flawed concept is better than not doing anything at all. One can correct a flawed concept and move on. Failure is considered a step towards success without loss of enthusiasm.

HUMAN RELATIONSHIP

Enthusiasm is really very infectious and tremendous moral-booster. You get the best out of people by giving them the freedom to act. But they must be made answerable for the results. It is not authority that people really want but it is accountability.

People get the best out of a person if they leave him alone. If they assume authority over him, many a time it may not work. Respect in an organisation flows from the demonstration of performance, intelligence, and knowledge by the individual.

Many achievements are not created by individual effort, but by collaborative, group level interactions. That needs respect and mutual esteem as the glue for cementing relationships that can be leveraged for creative value-addition. Ability to manage people is a key factor behind success. One should not only empower his people but also keep them motivated.

WAYS TO STAY SMART

The following would help to always stay smart:

(1) Continue to study even new subjects. This not only gives a substantial knowledge but also forces one to be open to new disciplines, new approaches and new methods.

(2) Review and Prioritise. This would enable to know: What were the things we should concentrate? What were the things we should improve? What were the things each of us needed to learn?

(3) Change with the Time. When you have a new assignment, ask yourself the question. What do I need to do, to be effective?

(4) Compare Expectations and Results. It is another key to continuous learning.

GOLDEN PRINCIPLES

If we can remember and act on the following, we will be able to make the circumstances more favourable to us than before and lead a happy and successful life.

(i) Respect the important person connected with the issue.

(ii) Have self-confidence. Mould yourself as a capable and suitable person.
(iii) Everyday, at the first instance, handle the most difficult job. Afterwards, you will experience happiness while dealing with comparatively easy ones.
(iv) Discipline your work.
(v) Don't be afraid of criticism. Criticise yourself frequently.
(vi) Be happy at other people's happiness and their victory. Study the procedures followed by those who achieved victory.
(vii) Don't fall into a wrong track because of dissatisfaction.
(viii) Be enthusiastic. It spreads from one to the other.
(ix) Don't be under the illusion that earning money alone is achieving victory.
(x) Do atleast one good work everyday.

THINKING PERSON

Even if there are unacceptable realities, a thinking person accepts the realities as those showing him the way. One who is ruled by excitement, frequently falls before he reaches his destination. A thinking person knows that proper way and beneficial way are not the same always. Instead of feeling happy at the mistakes committed by others, a thinking person tries to find out what new things can be learnt from that. One who finds fault with others and does not learn from others' mistakes, commits the same mistakes again and again.

A thinking person knows when to speak and when not to speak. A thinking person knows when to work and when to wait. A thinking person has the humility to recognise the wisdom in others. A thinking person weighs the words and talks carefully. A thinking person accepts that reality is more important than his total experience.

A thinking person is best illustrated in the following story:

An aged man lived in surrounding area of Jaipur. He wanted to cultivate his garden but it was hard work for him. His son, who would have helped him, was in prison! The aged man wrote a letter to his son explaining his situation:

"Dear Son, I am really feeling bad because I won't be able to cultivate my garden this year. I hate to miss because your mother always loved planting time. I am just getting too old to cultivate and plant the garden. All my troubles would be over, if you were here. I know you would excavate the plot for me but unfortunately, you are in prison. Your Dad."

The aged man received this telegram shortly:

"For God's sake, Dad don't dig up the garden! That's where, I buried the guns!!" Your Son." Next day, a dozens of local police with their officers came and dug up the entire garden without finding any guns. Astonished! Aged man wrote another letter to his son informing him what happened and asked what to do next.
His Son's reply was: "Go ahead and plant your garden. Dad, . . . it's the best I could do by my thinking mind for you."

WHAT DOES IT TAKE TO BE SOMEONE WHO MAKES A DIFFERENCE

In the present competitive environment, we find specific companies, which are perceived as performing better than others by the public in general and customers and investors, in particular. This may be because of quality products and services; or the image of the company perceived by the general public? The answer is a combination of these, coupled with the profile of the corporate leader.

These leaders are well qualified, have high conceptual ability, and. excellent corporate track record. Of course, companies are run by a group and not an individual, yet, it is this key person who makes the difference.

In our country, among the two types of Manager's—skilled and highly skilled, the second category makes a difference, as they are able to ensure that their organisation is able to perform well even in adverse conditions.

Based on interaction, three types of innovations in an organisation give certain companies an edge to perform—

(i) Technological Innovations where the primary objective is to reduce the unit cost of the goods sold.
(ii) Role Innovations, where efforts are being made to gainfully uitilise the potential of each employee.
(iii) Systems Innovations, where information is available and used for timely and quick decision making.

Some of the essential common qualities are:

(i) Very good interpersonal skills.
(ii) Excellent oral communication skills.
(iii) High commitment on improving technical and managerial knowledge.
(iv) Ability to analyse the market opportunity, strategically plan and take timely decisions.
(v) Good time management in developing time to work, self development, professional activity and friends.

LEADING CHANGE ... POWER OF PEOPLE

INITIATE: Starting, stopping or shifting the focus of activities according to the needs of the work unit.

INQUIRE: Gathering pertinent facts and data, whether through other people or other information sources.

ADVOCATE: Presenting one's own thoughts and intentions clearly and candidly.

RESOLVE CONFLICTS: Handling conflicts in a positive manner.

MAKE DECISIONS: Making decisions alone or in a combined effort with others.

CRITIQUE: Looking at current and past activities to determine ways of improving future endeavours.

WHAT MAKES A FIRM TO STAY AHEAD

Is it clarity of vision, a sense of purpose, the talent of the people involved, its marketing strategies, or a combination of all these?

The framework comprises the first three elements of strategy, structure and systems, considered the 'hardware' of success. The next four—Style, Staff, Skill and Shared Values—are the 'software'. The software elements would mean: (i) Employees in that company share a common style of behaving and thinking; (ii) Company has hired able people as staff, trained and assigned the right jobs to them; (iii) Employees have mastered the skills needed to carry out company strategy; (iv) Employees share the organisation's guiding values and missions.

The search for supremacy ends only in its achievement. Inspite of ever-changing and difficult market conditions, these companies have stood strong, evolved and excellent.

19

The Successful Manager—The Hero of the Organisation

Condensed knowledge is vision and vision is knowledge and the progress is its most important product. Organisation must have manager in order to function. Management is concerned with monitoring, facilitating and directing the accomplishment of organizational objectives. The systematic assessment of an organisation activities, evaluating performance, identifying areas of improvement and developing plans for future action are the key to success. Understanding tomorrow's challenges and developing the skills to tackle them is equally important.

HOW TO KEEP THE VISION ALIVE, TO ACHIEVE SUCCESS

We must put all our efforts together to nurture managers of the future, who by the vision, perseverance, skills, team spirit and conviction will become the shining stars of the corporate and business horizon. We are in a time, where there can be no set rules for leadership and vision. However, the following are the ELEMENTS FOR KEEPING THE VISION ALIVE TO ACHIEVE SUCCESS:

(i) **Use Strategic Language,** a common vocabulary of expression that everyone understands in the organisation.

(ii) **Keep Strategy Simple and Specific** to ensure that everyone can understand and contribute to it.

(iii) **Manage Participation** by clearly defining roles and creating opportunity to involve the key contributors. Move people towards shared vision.

(iv) **Motivate the entire workforce** to keep the vision an ongoing, energetic influence.

(v) **CEO's Involvement** at each important step to keep vision alive.

We must change our vision, mindset, work ethics, destiny and value drastically, keeping in mind the global outlook and to match with future challenges to win. Keep revising your vision periodically since growth has no limit. When you dream it, you can do it.

WHAT ARE THE BASIC TASKS OF A MANAGER

In order to achieve sustained superior performance, the foundations of every manager's job constitutes the following basic tasks.

(i) **Shaping the Work Environment:** Determine the company's performance standards, business concepts and human values.

(ii) **Setting Strategy:** Actively finding ways to give customers, the better values than competitors.

(iii) **Allocating Resources:** Concentrating resources on opportunities for gaining a competitive edge or atleast improving continuously on existing status of the company.

(iv) **Developing Employees:** Personal job review—Personally leading periodic meetings—and to appreciate the talent- rather than delegating the process to department heads.

(v) **Building the Organisation:** Looking ways for finding the right match between people and purpose to do things.

(vi) **Overseeing Operations:** Producing sound plans, spotting and responding to problems and opportunities quickly; in order to meet goals.

WHAT GOOD PRACTICES MANAGERS ADOPT

(i) **Listen:** Listening is critical, when you make important decisions and resolving disputes.

(ii) **Be Objective:** Identify with performance, not personality.

(iii) **Seek Several Opinions:** To see true picture that will enable you to communicate and evaluate more effectively.

(iv) **Be the Model:** Set the example in professionalism, work ethic, integrity and morals.

(v) **Delegate:** Let people take responsibility to grow and avail another chance.

(vi) **Audit Performance:** When you give an assignment, monitor the progress to make it meaningful.

(vii) **Develop People:** Plan for development of your subordinates.

(viii) **Like People:** Like your people to manage.

(ix) **Recognize Your Limits:** Capitalise on your strengths.

(x) **Accelerate Growth:** Recognize our weaknesses and correct them; act with a clear vision, an action plan and a determination to attain every opportunity to accelerate economic growth of the organisation.

THE IMPORTANT CHARACTERISTICS OF A SUCCESSFUL MANAGER

The characteristics of a successful manager are related to attitude as under.

(i) Understanding : Attitude of Understanding.

(ii) Anticipation : Sense of anticipation for good things yet to come in future.

(iii) Expectations : Expect to bring out the best in people.

(iv) Confidence : Self-confidence and develop confidence in people.

(v) Patience : Admire people who have patience.

(vi) Humility : Realization of and an emphasis of the importance of others. It's not putting myself down but really lifting-up others and recognising the value of others.

(vii) Belief : Anticipation and expectation of faith which is really belief and confidence.

WHAT IS THE PRIME IMPORTANCE AREA OF AN EFFECTIVE MANAGER

"Effectiveness is neither an ability nor a talent but it is a habit, a practice, a self-discipline that must be learned." Each company has its own work environment which dictates its managers—how to respond to the problem and opportunities. These elements are:

(a) **Prevailing Performance Standards** that set the step and quality of people's efforts.

(b) **Business Concepts** that defines what the company stands for and how it operates.

(c) **People Concepts and Values** that determines what it likes to work.

You need to raise your performance expectations from everyone for long term success. The success depends mainly on skillful handling of problems and opportunities in order to achieve your organization's objectives. Don't fear failure.

The Effective Manager

(i) Pulls for neither work nor management nor self-interest exclusively but rather for the interests of the organization.

(ii) Possesses human skills- understanding, supportiveness, ability to communicate clearly, ability to work with others.

(iii) Possesses conceptual skills—understanding the big picture, ability to organize, ability to make predictions and solve problems.

(iv) Has influence-get ideas and recommendations accepted by superiors, is supported and respected by upper management.

(v) Favours neither the task nor the worker exclusively but is concerned with both to the appropriate degree.

(vi) Uses scientific approaches when needed but also trusts an intuitive sense.

(vii) Looks for ways to build developmentally. Encourage sharing knowledge.

(viii) Perceives himself or herself as a manager rather than a worker and identifies self as a team member.

(ix) Identifies with the company objectives.

(x) Maintains a stable sense of value about self and society.

(xi) Spend their time in getting really important things done.

(xii) Prioritise really important things out of their "To-Do List" and then do scheduling of the day.

(xiii) Eliminate non-essential things such as—

(a) Spend time doing those things which are getting greater value.

(b) Expand work only to time available for completion instead of being perfectionist to consume lot of time. To do it in less time makes all the difference in work.

(xiv) Handle each piece of paper only once and categorise them in.....

(a) Things on which you can take immediate action.

(b) Pending category for example-paper pertaining to meeting next week- put them in appropriate file and make a note for same in your calendaring system.

(c) Paper which immediately goes into the waste paper basket.

(d) "Article to be read"—keep in separate folder to read whenever convenient.

(xv) Plan ahead to complete the job systematically and in time. Take time to sharpen your axe to get more output than planned.

(xvi) Don't place themselves under the limitations. We need to expect the best from our people.

(xvii) Man becomes what he thinks about all day. Change your mind attitude to achieve more and expect to get maximum from your people. Bible says, "As the person believes in his heart so is he". Raise your self-concept that you can accomplish more. Always expect the best out of your people to increase their performance.

MANAGERIAL STYLES AND SKILLS

Over and above the experience, both the managerial styles and skills are critically important in order to achieve the goals of increased efficiency and satisfaction. These are reflected below:

[A] Managerial Style

(i) Good enough is not enough—one must strive for the outstanding performance.

(ii) Trying hard is not enough, results only count.

(iii) Enough excellence is not enough. If you want to survive in competition, always try to achieve super-excellence.

(iv) It is good to have a healthy dissatisfaction with things that have always been done in a routine way.

(v) Treat everyone fairly but not the same. What you need to motivate one person may not be the same for another person.

(vi) It pays to care and to care deeply about your individual efforts, your unit/organisation, your colleagues, superiors, subordinates; your clients, your investors and customer satisfaction.

(vii) We do not need shooting stars but we need employees who are able to improve performance day after day, week after week, month after month continuously to handle their responsibilities.

(viii) Motivation and leadership are the necessities for success.

(ix) Allow yourself only to be the best, and nothing else.

(x) Enough is not enough. Perceptions are as important as reality.

(xi) Keep your dreams biggest, ambitions high commitment deeper and efforts greater for achievements, backed by your confidence, courage and conviction to achieve even the impossible.

(xii) Growth has no limit. Keep revising your vision. When you dream it, you can do it. Don't give-up courage but convert your dreams into reality.

(xiii) Meeting the deadlines is not enough but beating the deadlines are the real expectations.

(xiv) Persue your goals even in the face of difficulties and make efforts to convert adversities into the opportunities.

(xv) Develop ability to convert your vision and big dreams into realities backed by your hold and perseverance.

(xvi) Develop employees to be the best, most talented, highly motivated; nurture and propel them to aim for continuous higher goals.

(xvii) Develop leadership qualities, foresight, excellence, modesty with capacity to motivate and trust people. Trust is a basic perquisite of doing business.

(xviii) Don't Forecast the future—but Create it.

(xix) Create new opportunities for growth through innovation and to carry out both "routine" and "non-routine" activities in response to changing needs and aspirations for organisation.

[B] Managerial Skills

For creating a sustainable, economically viable organisation, the following requisite skills provide everybody a fair chance for success.

(i) Team Building and to give way to an enlightened approach that taps the energies of employees, both individually and in teams.

(ii) Your view point is shaped by your view. Where you stand, depends upon where you sit.

(iii) Success comes to those with high tolerance for ambiguity and frustration.

(iv) Think big, Think differently, Think fast and aim for the best, since ideas are no one's monopoly.

(v) Think ahead of others and take steps to get the right information and expert assistance.

(vi) Maintain ambitious initiatives to do with changing mindsets, attitudes, policies and preferences.

(vii) Work with perfection and determination to ensure that success will follow.

(viii) Simplify the complex, see the complexities of the simple. The winner lays stress on KISS ("Keep It Simple Stupid").

(ix) Treat unimportant details and records. Maintain and retain only the important details and records.

(x) Develop your subordinates to take responsibilities of senior position. Launch one initiative after another.

(xi) Often, the only certainty is the uncertainty. You will have to take action and make decisions with facts and information, available considerably limited.

(xii) Control but don't overcontrol. Let those closest to the situation have considerable freedom to act and exercise their intelligence, creativity and growth potential.

(xiii) Innovate or continuously improve. Being satisfied with everything as it is, will result sure to fall behind competitors, within as well as outside your organisation.

(xiv) To develop skills to stimulate organisational innovation. Make innovation happen to win the market competition as well as value creation.

(xv) Imagination is more important than knowledge. Be

a INNOVATOR, who can see what everybody else sees, but think of what no body else think.

(xvi) Neither all data are information nor all information comes from data; also not all data or information are important.

(xvii) Make sure that your base is solid before you expand.

(xviii) Hire the right people and offer them multiple routes to achieve success. Create a learning environment that inspires free flow of new ideas by building bridges of understanding.

(xix) You can't avoid making decisions for long duration. If you do so, time, events and competitors will overcome and overtake you.

WHAT IS THE DIFFERENCE BETWEEN STYLE OF MANAGING AS COMPARED TO STYLE OF LEADING

	Style of Managing	*Style of Leading*
(i)	Directing Others	— Guiding/developing
(ii)	Competing	— Collaborating
(iii)	Using hierarchy	— Using network
(iv)	Consistency	— Diversity/flexibility
(v)	Slow decision making-requiring permission	— Fast decision making-using judgement
(vi)	Risk averse	— Risk taking
(vii)	Individual contributor	— Team player
(viii)	Being managed	— Self management
(ix)	People as expense	— People as asset.

HOW TO IMPROVE YOUR EMPLOYEES LOYALTY OR COMMITMENT

The steps can be taken to ensure that the goals are shared by all your employees.

(a) Make your goals so clear and simple that every employee can understand them and do something about them everyday.
(b) Be fully committed to your own goals.
(c) Train and retrain your employees to improve skills so that they help you to make your goals a reality and improve their performance by building capabilities.
(d) Communicate clearly, visibly and constantly, the information on the progress at every level on its chosen goals. This creates harmony by connecting people to each other.
(e) Trust your employees to do the right things. Just give them the opportunity and they will reward you well. Value people's input and get commitment through participation.
(f) Meet challenging and exciting goals to deliver high quality results from the motivated and competent employees.
(g) Give employees a share in the financial benefits of your success. Commitment can work wonders; making the impossible attainable.

If you do it, you help to make your company competitive, by your efforts to improve productivity and efficiency. You help to satisfy customer's need and keep good reputation of your company by meeting critical schedules and quality standards. You become an example to the organisation, community and the people around you by fulfilling your responsibility to organisation and employees. You need to recognise that managing is a quite different skill from many other kinds of work. You need the passion to win and win everytime which can be achieved by improving performance ethics to the benefit of the shareholders, employees, customers and community and above all, to create wealth on a sustainable basis for the organisation. People say that the circumstances changes frequently but real manager change the circumstances. Keep yourself nurture with winner thoughts which will add value to your personality. The positive energy within you will grow and others with you will feel enriched. You will get firmly established even under adversities. There is an important reason for writing things down because writing crystallizes thought and thought produces actions. **You don't just think it but ink it and do it so that you will be well on your way to become a High Performing Successful Manager.**

20

Leadership in Management—The Trend Setter

PART I

INTRODUCTION

Leaders are driven by their vision, ambitions and goals. A significant factor that can either make or break an organisation is the leadership. The success of an organisation in this competitive era depends largely on how well it caters to its customers. In order to keep pace with the latest development, the position of the organisational head as leader has become highly imperative. The effectiveness of leaders depends upon their capabilities to maintain continuity in the progress and success of their organisation in the light of transition taking place within the system. Leadership with main inputs of behavioral modifications by the organisational head is emerging as an alternative concept to manage challenges of future.

In every endeavour, only one or a few persons are recognised despite the fact that the achievement is a consequence of the contributions made by many people. Why is it so? There is something special and it resembles superiority, dominance, uniqueness, love, recognisation, precedence, forwardness, drive, influence, status, and charisma. The most important aspect in any definition is "influence". A leader creating the group's or organisational missions and outlining the strategy for attaining them, has to influence different persons in different groups in different ways and styles. Thus, the excellence of a leader depends upon the capability to deal with different types of relationships successfully. The excellence, thus, is the outcome of harassing and harmonising the energies and interests of people of all groups with whom a leader transacts to achieve the common total organisational goals and objectives.

THE INFLUENCE OF LEADERSHIP

ONE MAN THAT MAKES DIFFERENCE IS THE LEADER. Five Pandavas against 100 Kauravas was a losing equation for Pandavas. But for one advantage, they have an advisor par excellence, whose advise gave invaluable insight to Pandavas into their people, resources, strengths and the environment on the battlefield. This helped them substantially to exploit all their strengths and change the entire course of war.

LEADERSHIP—THE CONCEPT

Effective leaders adapt only that style of functioning which suits the given situation. If they fail to do so, they are termed as 'biased". A leader functions as the situation demands but also has the capability of changing a situation by exerting influence on group members, motivating them to useful channels by bringing a change in their ideologies and attitudes.

DEVELOPING LEADERSHIP

There is a need to rethink on how to make decisions, solve problems, plan for the future, communicate successfully, allocate time efficiently, manage politics and get the most of other people as an effective leaders. It is now that the position of organisational heads have become quite demanding as they are the ones who are expected to lay down good systems and workable procedures within their workplaces, re-organising their thinking, behaviour and styles of functioning. This is possible only when head as leader initiate the process by understanding their workplaces and people.

Field Marshal Sam Manekshaw convincingly expressed his views about leadership that "Profession competence, moral, physical courage, absolute impartiality and loyalty are the ingredients of good leadership. What we lack as a nation is discipline and that is the most essential quality to lead others."

LEADERSHIP TRAITS

The Leaders are higher in honesty, wealth creation, wiseness, intelligence, ambition, motivation, drive, self-confidence and several other traits. In addition, successful leaders appear to be high in flexibility—the ability to adapt their style to the follower's needs and to the requirements of specific situations.

The honesty is of prime importance which eventually pays in long run. It reinforces trust and loyalty as well as love and respect. Therefore, it is essential to cultivate the habit of honesty. A relevant story is quoted below:

There was an honest wood-cutter. While cutting the wood, his axe fell into the river and he started crying. Eventually, Jal Devta appeared and agreed to help him. He dipped into river and brought up a gold axe but wood-cutter refused to accept, that it does not belongs to him. Next time, brought up a silver axe and again he refused to accept. Third time, brought up iron axe and the wood-cutter was indeed obliged as it was his own. The Jal Devta insisted wood-cutter to accept all three and he was delighted.

Besides, Leaders are supposed to be higher in wealth creation and wiseness as under:

अर्थसिद्धिं परामिच्छन्, धर्ममेवादिश्चरेत।
न हि धर्मादपेत्यर्थः स्वर्गलोकादिवामृतम्।।

महाभा./उद्योग/37/48

यदि मनुष्य श्रेष्ठ धन की प्राप्ति करना चाहता है, तो उसे आरम्भ से ही धर्म का पालन करना चाहिए। धन धर्म से पृथक नहीं किया जा सकता; जैसे स्वर्ग लोक से अमृत पृथक नहीं हो सकता। भावार्थ यह है कि धर्मपूर्वक कमाया हुआ धन ही स्थायी और सुख का साधन होता है।

If a man desires to get ideal riches, he should act according to morality from the beginning. Riches can never be gained without morality, as the nector comes from the heaven only.

* * *

अभयं यस्य भूतेभ्यः, सर्वेषामभयं यतः।
स वै परिणतप्रज्ञः, प्रख्यातो मनुजोत्तमः॥

महाभा./उद्योग/63/19

प्राणियों से जिसे भय नहीं है और प्राणी भी जिस से भयभीत नहीं होते, वही व्यक्ति बुद्धिमान् तथा प्रसिद्ध पुरुषोत्तम है।

One that is not afraid of others and neither are others afraid of him, such a person is called wise and the best of the human beings.

LEADERSHIP INFLUENCE

Influence is the relationship which exists between the influencer and the influenced. The influencer is the leader and the influenced cover: 1. Purpose 2. Followers 3. Competitors, 4. Opponents (enemies), 5. Superiors and 6. Customers (Beneficiaries).

POSITIVE INFLUENCING is based on love, sympathy, empathy, and sacrifice shared by the leader with the influence. On the other hand, a leader also administers threat, intimidation, punishment, reprimand and humiliation on the influenced, which can be termed as NEGATIVE INFLUENCING.

The major source of inspiration a leader derives is from his purpose. It creates a consciousness in mind, a principle of action, a sense of belongingness and meaningfulness to the endeavour. The purpose may be selfish or selfless, social or political, money or power or in a combination of a few or all. A sincere purpose makes a leader to face the challenge instead of running away to escape from crisis.

Purpose

No other engine is powerful that can drive an organisation towards excellence than the achievable purpose widely shared. Purpose generates energy.

Followers

A major task of a leader is to create an environment in which he can operate and implement his action plans in order to fulfil his visionary purposes. Towards this, he has to behave in such a way that the followers should feel total "confidence" so as to surrender themselves to the leader and follow the commands. The image that a leader creates on the followers would be that there is a person who can fulfil their aspirations, who can protect them in crisis and who can meet their needs. This confidence has very great potentiality and it can move the mountains. To create confidence, a leader should have faith in himself that he can do so and also in the abilities of his followers. Providing minimum requirements, facilities and comforts to his men in order to make them and keep them fit to do the desired job is one of the important duties of a leader in creating a favourable environment.

Competitors

A leader may be very effective or efficient in influencing his own followers. But there would still be others who would be ready to throw out the leader with the first available chance. Even among followers, there could emerge a challenge for his leadership.

Opponents

A major source of energy a leader gets is from one of

the many dimensions of the purpose, which is related to conquering, defeating or overpowering the opponents and enemies. Who is this opponent? An individual becomes an enemy due to the fact that he has done some personal harm or due to the ideological differences. Whenever a person wants to reverse the existing order, custom or tradition of another leader, then they become enemies to each other. A brand name of a company is an enemy to another brand in same product.

Superiors

A leader has to influence indirectly the superiors with appropriate styles and activities. Though a leader's major task is to influence the followers and opponents, the influencing of superiors also contribute to his excellence to a great deal.

Customers

A leader should understand and realise that everyone, both within and outside the organisation, who supply inputs, material, technology information, perform the job of others and add values for the organisations as customers. The tangibles expectation of customers are like specification, conformance, reliability, price and delivery, and also the intangibles like warmth, genuineness, courtesy, unconditional positive regard, politeness, helpful attitude conformance, reliability, price and delivery, empathy, openness, affection, concern, sympathy, equity and cooperation. The leader plays a critical role in sharing the intangibles expectations of customers.

DECISION MAKING

The most appropriate style of decision making are made on the basis of the quality of the decision required and the degree to which it is important for followers to accept and be committed to the decisions being made.

UNDERSTANDING THE WORKPLACE

The foremost step requires an understanding the existing situation, resources and people. This could be followed by an analysis of probable factors that will bring the desired results and facilitate in tuning strategies in accordance with the requirements and priorities of the organisation. This exercise calls for diagnosis of problems, identification of particular needs, assessment of the limitations and resources. Based on such an assessment, the leader can then establish their own priorities, goals, standards and even targets for their organisations.

UNDERSTANDING OTHERS AND SELF

Understanding others is crystalising the managerial competence of a leader, if one endeavours to exist in a system. This however, requires an examination of:

- Why behaviour of others disturbs me?
- Why someone tends to make me feel good?
- Why do people react in certain ways they do?
- What are their assumptions and expectations from me?
- What do they think of themselves?
- What are their general attitude towards life, work and overall situation prevailing around them?

These concerns tend to expose the viewpoints/opinions of people, with whom the leader works and their motivation as well as behaviour and overall relationship with peers, subordinates and superiors.

Developing a positive outlook is the most fundamental constituent to bring about changes in the situation. One must be able to develop the mental attitude that nothing is impossible.

CREATING ORGANISATION-BASED VISION

On the basis of an analysis of organisations and people therein, development of an organisation-based vision and plan of improvement can be practised by leader in one form or the other. The Leaders need to sharpen, develop their own vision and make it coherent, respectable and legitimate for others. Most of the dynamic and committed organisational heads do have a vision for their institutions.

TEAM BUILDING

This is an most important function of the efficient and effective Leader. TEAM WORK is the ability to work together towards a common vision. TEAM SPIRIT is the ability to direct individual achievement towards organisational objectives. By working together, ordinary people can perform extraordinary excellence to attain the common goals and objectives of the total organisation. "WORKING TOGETHER MEANS WINNING TOGETHER".

EXCHANGING AND SHARING VISION

The organisational heads can bring changes in their work situations only if they exchange ideas and opinions, share information with their colleagues. Sharing of organisational values is highly important if intentions of the leader are to make the staff cooperate with endeavour for improvement.

CULTIVATING A CLIMATE OF RISK TAKING

This part although quite vital for bringing improvements in the system, has not been taken up seriously. There is a fear that one might have to do away with the job if (s)he takes decisions that is not in the taste of superiors. This culture has to be cultivated. A leader must be able to take risks while taking decisions, which perhaps could be challenged also. An over cautious or a timid approach will never pay.

CONCLUSION

People are the prime movers who make institutions function in the most effective or ineffective manner. In

order to lock the organisation in a renewal process on a continuous basis, the organisational leader will have to follow a dynamic approach. While performing tasks, one needs to understand the mechanisms by which this can be managed in a more efficient manner. An efficient leader approach rests upon "Doing Right Things" always. However, they cannot function in isolation. They will have to constitute teams and adapt positive dynamics to manage the group for becoming an acceptable member of the whole organisation team.

A true leader knows that in the long run, nothing in this universe belongs to him. His own existence is for a temporary period and everything that he holds is for a given period of time as a trustee.

PART II

"The first opinion that is formed of a leader intelligence is based on the quality of the men, he has around him. When they are competent, enthusiastic, loyal with their total commitment and positive attitude, he can always be considered wise since he has been able to recognise their competence and keep them loyal."

WHO IS LEADER

A leader is a person who attracts and selects an outstanding team, train and coaches them and obtain their total commitment to the organisational goals. A leader has to be a visionary. He has to be able to see what others cannot. He has to be able to take risk and must have the courage to stand-by his convictions. He must have the intelligence to remain open to new philosophies. **In a nutshell —the commitment, passion, purpose and belief makes a leader effective.** A leader takes the first step towards something and deeply cares the same in a way that others wish to follow. **The wisdom is knowing what to do. The skill is knowing how to do it. The success is in implementing it.**

Leadership involves focusing the efforts of a group of people towards a common goal and enabling them to work

together as team. The importance of the leader is in team work, team building and team maintenance as a whole. The primary responsibility of leader is to define the objective and clear goals. Achieving the aim is the ultimate test of leadership. All leaders are team-builders. They use their wisdom to choose the right people as team members, out of the collection of possible members which is the first principal of team success.

Leader fix-up specific good targets which are relevant, time-bound, measurable, realistic, challenging, attainable and agreed. Achieving the task, building and maintaining the team and developing the individual is the core responsibility of the leader. **Leader has to perform the key functions like planning, initiating, controlling, supporting, informing and evaluating.**

(i) **BE ENTHUSIASTIC!** When you have enthusiasm and commitment, you have got a lot to be excited.

(ii) **BE POSITIVE!** Feed your mind with positive mental attitude.

(iii) **BE INVOLVED!** Attend discussions and meetings.

(iv) **BE SUCCESSFUL!** Think and talk as if the success you want were yours already. Success breeds success, enjoy it.

LEADERSHIP IN MANAGEMENT

A company can flourish by accomplishing its goals through developing leaders in all aspects, at all levels of its business. Leadership is neither a charisma nor a set of personality traits. Effective leaders think through the organisation's mission and then clearly define and establish it. They set goals that are compatible with the mission, then set priorities, as well as set and maintain standards. Effective leaders consider leadership as a responsibility rather than rank and privilege. They hold themselves accountable when things go wrong. They encourage strong associates and subordinates never viewing their trumphs as threats. Finally, effective leaders earn trust with their professed beliefs.

The management goals must be to develop each individual with specific strengths and knowledge to deliver the desired results. Thus the task is not only to manage people but to lead them. Management must be operational to focus on results and performance, across the entire economic chain. Leadership is all about results. Leaders can go from being average to extraordinary and from being good to being great. They understand that continued improvement in leadership ability makes a substantial difference in the results, which they want to attain. **Focus on results, managing for excellence, interpersonal skills, leading organisational changes, getting a grip on creativity, group decision making, problem solving, team effectiveness, motivation and converting 'me' to 'we' negotiating are some of the essential traits; needs to be developed as demanded by the new challenges of today's fast-moving business. A leader should command respect rather than demand it.**

THE NECESSITY TO LEAD

The secret to success in leadership development is ultimately about self-development to fulfill promises. **The exemplary leadership practices are as under:**

(i) Model the way.
(ii) Inspire a shared vision.
(iii) Challenge the process.
(iv) Enable others to act.
(v) Encourage the entire team members.

People do not feel their presence, when true leaders are amongst them. A leader's value is not only determined by a set of guiding beliefs but also by ability to act on these beliefs. The following specific action steps can be used to accomplish extraordinary things from others:

(i) Find your voice by clarifying your personal values.
(ii) Set the example by aligning actions with shared values.
(iii) Envision the future by imagining exciting and

distinguish possibilities.

(iv) Enlist others in a common vision by appealing to shared aspirations.

(v) Search for opportunities by seeking innovative ways to change, grow and improve.

(vi) Experiment and take risks by constantly generating wins and learning from mistakes.

(vii) Foster collaboration by promoting cooperative goals and building trust.

(viii) Strengthen others by sharing power and discretion.

(ix) Recognise contributions by showing appreciation for individual excellence.

(x) Celebrate the values and victories by creating a spirit of commonness.

Belief in yourself and belief in others since everyone wants success. Belief 'you can succeed' creates strong confidence in you. 'I can' is a powerful sentence. The gap between what a man thinks as compared to what he actually achieve is very small. But action never occurs until you believe, you can do it. Therefore, first you must believe that you can do it and succeed.

INDIVIDUAL LEADERSHIP SKILLS

Question: How I would lead, if I have no authority? Would co-workers follow me voluntarily because of my good ideas, strength of character and concern for their welfare?

Answer: No one has a monopoly on ideas. People who rely on rank are not true leaders. Full commitment to a task cannot be compelled but it must be inspired.

ARE YOU HAVING LEADERSHIP TROUBLE

Find out, if you are a true leader by seeing, if you possess these qualities:

(i) Leaders start projects by asking "What has to be done?" instead of "What do I need?"

(ii) Leaders ask "What do I have to do to make a real

contribution?" The answer best suits the leader's strengths and the needs of the project.

(iii) Leaders continually ask "What are my organization's purpose and objective?" "What qualifies as acceptable performance?"

(iv) Leaders never ask "Do I like or dislike this employee?" But they won't tolerate poor performance.

Encourage shared thinking by which decisions will be faster, more innovative, matured, stronger and of greater value. Get the right people around you to put your decisions into action.

HOW TO SHARPEN YOUR ABILITY TO ASK QUESTIONS

In this connection, I would like to cite the specific example from Ramayana as to why the ability to ask questions is essential. King Ravana of Sri Lanka alone was a very wise man equivalent to ten. But his ten wisest heads were not open, when his sister Sarupnakha came crying, putting allegation that Laxmana cut her nose without any valid reason. Ravana, confident with his superpower did not ask her right questions to find facts and verify the correctness. He neither investigate what went wrong nor find out what happened, when, how and why to arrive at a correct conclusion. Even without enquiry of the root cause, he believed distorted story of Sarupnakha and become short tempered. Had Ravana asked relevant questions the Sri Lanka war with Rama and its consequences could have been avoided. Perhaps, we would have handled it differently. The moral of the story is that we must think all thinkables and unthinkables through all our senses and use our mind to its full potential instead of taking shortcuts and creating endless problems by anger.

The important and difficult job is never to find the right answer, but it is to find the right questions. **Leaders plant seeds of change around them with their questions, cultivate**

these seeds with constant enquiry and harvest the results by asking whether the change is working as desired. Leaders know that **organisation must continuously make small improvements to maintain and grow their market positions.** The questions that illuminate and inspire can make all the difference to become more productive to raise warn alarm for organisation to be prepared for sudden and permanent change. Focus on the following elements to remove the obstacles:

(i) AWARENESS: What are the most important things you need to know? Are you looking for facts? How much information are you willing to share?

(ii) ABILITY: Make sure you are asking a person who has the expertise and authority to answer your questions.

(iii) ATMOSPHERE: Give careful consideration to when and where you ask your questions.

(iv) ATTITUDE: Your questions to the respondent's—then really listen to the answers you receive.

(v) ANSWER: Are the responses you have received verifiable? Did all your questions get answered?

(vi) APPRECIATION: Even if the answers you receive don't meet your needs, demonstrate your gratitude anyway. Such appreciation can encourage others. Moreover, be sure to explain your questions in a way that gives people a reason to help you in the future.

(vii) ACTION: Make sure your questions have real-world consequences.

It is not doing the things we like to do, but liking the things we have to do, that makes life blessed. A good leader inspires men with confidence in him but a great leader inspires them with confidence in themselves.

Leader's respect remains in the hearts and minds of those who work for him. Both the praise and criticism are essential at the right time and in the right place. Honesty, integrity, moral courage and fairness are essential to make better and more effective teams. As a matter of fact, team work is the by-product of good leadership.

21

How to Achieve Sure Success—A Few Tips

PART I

"The success is the ability to go from failure to failure without loosing enthusiasm." said Winston Churchill. Success knows no boundaries and leader must have boundless enthusiasm. The first step towards success is a great dream. "If you dare to dream, there is a whole world to win."

Everyone has potential. If you think good, good will happen, but if you think negative, so will happen. **The most important aspect is to establish faith in yourself, by repeatedly attempting to achieve the goals, as the steps towards success. Do not fear for failure.** No one can make you feel inferior without your consent. Thomas Alva Edition was discouraged by telling that **"You have failed 10000 times, why to try again?" The answer was "I atleast know 10000 ways, it cannot work." The positive thoughts are vital factor, if you want to succeed in any endeavour. If you aim at excellence, you can achieve it.**

Business now is at a turning point. Everything in our world is changing faster than ever before. But most of us are clueless about what is causing change, how it might effect them and most importantly what to do above it? **The survival is not enough and we need to evolve the same**

way that nature evolves to flourish in times of change. Fortune favours the bold. The time demands more innovation, more competition and more changes. It won't go away but will increase gradually. Therefore, we need to learn how to evolve. **Change does not have to be enemy. We must start by-passing our fear for change by constantly training our people to make small changes. The change starts with you ... the employee. This is the way the organisation can drive to change faster and faster, to produce extraordinary results, to dominate markets by embracing the change that will come inevitably.**

What experience has taught us, the most about successful leadership? It is a matter of setting right example. Opportunity has a new destination, when the leader unfolds a new vision for journey through his experience, commitment and guidance. **It is not enough to dream. It's important to build a sustainable base for those dreams to come true.** In order to see the light of the day, we must expand our talent pool which must be loved, nurtured and rewarded to make magic happen.

We must not confuse **"Excellence"** with **"Perfection". Perfection is unattainable. In fact, perfection is a journey. It does not stop at any definite target. Once goals are set, the targets are achieved. Then targets are revised and the journey continues. But excellence is achievable with enough concerted efforts.** If you strive for excellence, you may not always succeed at leading but you will certainly succeed at living whether you have an army of followers in your wake or you are alone. Therefore, whatever you do, do it with excellence. The crises actually helps you to lead and inspire others, to rise to the challenges and bring-out the best in them. **You can't win alone but you will feel yourself lucky, if your team-mates are better, smarter and faster than you since they would take care of the rest. Building good team is everyday affair in sports and same should be followed in business.** There is another example of Boris Becker who became world tennis champion at the age of seventeen. Next year during the initial rounds, he lost in a tennis match. The journalists rushed to him and excitedly asked several questions. Boris Becker answered "Friends, it was only a tennis match! No one died on the tennis court! I lost and a better player won!!" The moral of the story is that whenever we fail, we should never forget that the failure is an event.

If you dare to take challenge in pursuit of excellence, you must dream nothing else but success. Can anyone define success? The interpretation of success differs from person to person. The following are the traits of successful people.

1. They identify their strengths. Have a strong desire to achieve certain goals and think..... "If there is a way, we will find it."
2. Their victory depends on positive thoughts, emotions and courage.
3. They have a passion of winning.
4. They have energy, create energy, show energy and spread energy with their boundless enthusiasm.
5. They have a vision and develop a creative concept to turn their vision into an attainable objective.
6. They decide a clearly defined goals on important and high return task to achieve improvement and value addition to make things easier, better, faster and cheaper.
7. They set priorities carefully and decide what is to be done first and what next.
8. They have no one-size-fits approach to it. It all depends on right person and right style for the right situation.
9. They plan in advance to explore all options and leave no stone unturned. Foresight is the essence of a successful event.
10. They communicate effectively with their target audience. This not only generates awareness but it also helps to bolster confidence for the sponsors.
11. They have the ultimate power of relationship. What really matters are the relationships that they have

created with their people?
12. They relax rigid control over their thinking process. They use chance factor in encouraging divergent ideas and search for different ways of looking at it. They keep enterprise energised in the face of adversity and ambiguity.
13. They identify their enemies and treat them before they could obstruct the process of success.
14. They generate creativity to arrive at appropriate idea and know when to ask for help and involve others in their plan.
15. They have ability to work collaboratively with others.
16. They have strong analytical skills.
17. They have ability to think innovatively.
18. They take proper decision quickly with full responsibility for their actions to achieve the objectives.
19. They persevere towards the objectives.
20. They have a clear ability to lead.
21. They have ability to identify and work constructively towards opportunities.
22. They encourage entrepreneurial thinking throughout their organisation.
23. They are not scared to delegate.
24. They have a drive for continuous self-improvement and a genuine interest in the development of others.
25. They are able to execute their plans well, being in regular touch with their team. They always check the flow of the events for continuous improvement during implementation.
26. They firmly believe that they can do it. They find a way in which it can be done and ensure to make it happen.
27. They love the organisation and binds their employees through the process of commitment.
28. They maximise employees contribution and commitment to create the winning organisation.
29. They see the victory in front of their eyes and

concentrate their mind to achieve the goals.

30. They take action and measure results to evaluate the final outcome which makes sense.
31. They celebrate success, when it comes their way.
32. They revise the targets, once the earlier targets are achieved and continue the journey of success.
33. They enrich the organisation's value to the customers, investors and employees.

As a matter of fact, THE VISION WITHOUT ACTION IS MERELY A DREAM. THE ACTION WITHOUT VISION IS MERELY PASSING TIME. THE VISION ALONGWITH ACTION CAN DELIVER THE DESIRED RESULTS. **Believe firmly that you can make a difference and it should reflect in all your actions and words.** Spell out your plan of success by predetermined goals. Get an idea of where you want to go and work on your goals. Then constantly check whether you are on the right track.

The success depends upon the right attitude of people. **People who think positively, always implement positive actions and get positive results.** If people have right attitude, they make best teams to work effectively towards achieving the desired goals and ensure success in their objectives. One can certainly make changes in the attitude, if you have desire to do that. The desire of doing best things comes from the heart and soul. If the heart and soul are full of desire to excel, one can certainly get excellence in life.

The success comes to an organisation that encourages value addition involving high aspiration, new ideas, merit, innovation, speed, openness, entrepreneurship, fairness in every transaction and putting the interests of the community, customers, investors, employees ahead of personal interest.

Let us take an opportunity to lift-up from runaway and get altitude. Play to win and work effectively to achieve high targets. Because winning means reaching the right depth of your own potential and utilising it to its fullest.

It is business on a high-stake, high risk, high profile event that is filled with uncertainty and ambiguity. Therefore, the clear-cut performance outcome now matters more than ever before. Let us avail an opportunity to recharge your batteries, learn new skills, attend to long-overlooked problems and improve strained relationship.

Emotion is the key that generates enthusiasm for performance of duties. Believe firmly, what is 'today' becomes 'yesterday' and what is 'tomorrow' becomes 'today'. Give your best today to perform your duty, in practising values and ethics, in fulfilling all your commitments. The best will certainly come to you. Remember! Success is a journey and not a destination.

ANNEXURE 'A'

Evaluation of your Understanding — "How to Achieve Sure Success?"

What does success mean to you personally? The following points reflects success for your own evaluation:

(i) Develop the habits of initiative and facing issues.

(ii) Dedicate your life for continuous learning and self-improvement.

(iii) Conduct in such a way that others develop confidence in you that you will maintain your promises.

(iv) Be one who knows how to improve and how to work with others. Apportion your time to do your best.

(v) Success demands human qualities such as love, honesty, humility, forgiveness, empathy etc.

(vi) Success means chalking out a programme for life and sticking to it steadfastly.

(vii) Success bestows self-respect and a feeling that you have made good use of all your opportunities.

(viii) Success is building one's self-respect by affirming the dignity of one's fellow beings.

(ix) Success is doing something good when, where and while you can.

(x) Success is becoming a possibility thinker—daring to

dream the impossible.

(xi) Success is never ending. It continues to produce new possibilities and sometimes new problems. Failure is also never final.

(xii) Successful people radiate a positive attitude.

(xiii) Successful people make choices that involve risks.

(xiv) Successful people understand that no one reaches to the top in a single-bound step.

(xv) Success is success only when it is continuous and qualitative.

ANALYSIS

Score one mark for every "Yes" answer. Your understanding "How to achieve sure success" is as under:

11 to 15 Marks:	Excellent
06 to 10 Marks:	Fair
01 to 05 Marks:	Poor

PART II

INTRODUCTION

Are you looking for challenges in your life? What makes a business successful? Are you trapped in an endless cycle of financial frustration? Why do some strategic decision work, while others flop? Do you want to avoid the blunders that leads to complete collapse? Do you want to overcome the challenges and constraints that exists in your way? What is your ultimate goal?

Fighting battles of life is inevitable and we fight a battle each hour/day/ month/year; so why not fight to always win? Nothing succeeds like success. We should never look for an escape route after getting into the battle but instead take on the enemy to always win. An enlightened individual mind is full of fragrant thoughts, emotions and actions to achieve the good deeds which spreads far and wide to always win. Each of us is blessed with certain talents and gifts that make us unique individuals.

Success is a matter of positive attitude. It is a matter of what you think, you are capable of. It is a matter of futuristic thinking, planning and doing things carefully. You know what you are, but not what you can become. Develop your ability to persist in the face of adversity. Do not afraid of growing slowly but be afraid of remaining stand still. Don't measure yourself by what you have accomplished but rather by what you should have accomplished with your abilities. Life is a reasonable adventure for the people with a passionate attitude to work as restless energetic for striving, seeking and enjoying challenges. **Failures are just stepping stones of success to heroic minds.** I would like to cite an example. Everyone who has ever played a card game, knows that there must be a winner as well as loser. We all play to win but we know well in advance that chances are 50-50 that we win or lose. There is an another example that a eminent person had suffered the defeats several times, whose age at the time of setback is indicated against each here below:

Particulars	*Age*
Failed in business	22
Defeated for legislature	23
Failed in business again	24
Wife died	26
Suffered a nervous breakdown	27
Defeated for Speaker	29
Defeated for Elector	31
Defeated for Congress	34
Defeated for Congress	39
Defeated for Senate	46
Defeated for Vice-President	47
Defeated for Senate	49
Elected President of the United States	51

How would you feel, if you had suffered the defeats as above? The above is the record of Abraham Lincoln, whose leadership earned a name and fame in the history of United States. There is no success without failure and everyone encounter failure in their life. The success and failure have the same root—the desire to achieve.

Confidence comes from being prepared. It is not what you do but how you do it, is more important. If you think you can, you are right. Be passionate about it. If you lack passion, then develop it to achieve success. You have success within you. Success depends upon how you react to unexpected opportunities. It is upto you to bring it out. In order to achieve success every individual and organisation needs right positive attitude, discipline, skills and knowledge. The most gifted person cannot blossom into a good achiever; without sound values, good habits and strict self-discipline. Therefore, overall development of the personality like physical, emotional, intellectual and spiritual will go a long way in enriching life to optimise performance.

An optimistic approach generates ideas which in turn leads to thoughts and to maintain happiness, the proper thoughts are important. When nothing seems to help, I go and look at a stone-cutter hammering away at his rock, perhaps ninety-nine times without showing a crack in it. Yet at the hundred hammer, it will split in two. I know it was not that blow that did it but all that had gone before. **Greatness lies in being able to convert available circumstances into favourable ones. Victory depends on the way, we tackle the issue. If you have the will and energy to take on the toughest, there is nothing difficult or impossible to achieve.** Do not get disheartened by defeat but develop enthusiasm to try again. Thomas Edition failed 9999 times and after many more such attempts invented the Electric Bulb in year 1879.

WINNERS VERSUS LOSERS

In order to achieve success, you need to develop winner's thoughts. The comparison of WINNERS Versus

LOSERS at a glance is given below:

Winners	*Losers*
• Always a part of the answer.	• Always a part of the problem.
• Always have a programme.	• Always has an excuse.
• Says "Let me do it for you."	• Says "That is not my job."
• Sees an answer for "every problem."	• Sees a problem in every answer.
• Says "It may be difficult but it is possible."	• Says "It may be possible but it is too difficult."

Impossible is just another word for challenge. It's kind of fun to do the impossibles. Where there is a human will,..............there is a way. No ifs. No buts. Now go ahead. Options available are......

Winners	*Losers*
Optimist	Pessimist
Success	Failure
Perform	Perish
Evolve	Perish
Innovate	Perish
Do	Die
Conquer	Die
Swim	Sink
Fight	Flight
Win	Lose
Now	Never
Hit	Miss
Shape Up	Shake Out
Step Up	Step Down
Get Better	Get Worst
Make	Break
Stay	Quit
Entry	Exit
Life	Death
Cash	Crash

We imagine, originate and generate the leading edge to turn our inspiration into reality. Don't you want to discover something new everyday? Decide the shape of things to come? Design a future that is smarter, better and more exciting than ever before? **You can do all as winners do and even more.** You can give your career the big boost, straight into a bigger, brighter future. You have your whole life ahead of you, so it is important to lay the right foundation. **Keep on trying till the good becomes the better and the better becomes the best.**

GOOD FRIENDS

Make good friends before you actually need them. You can freely share your inner thoughts and exchange ideas with them. They will encourage and inspire you to move forward overcoming the challenges. They will create enthusiasm in you, when you are in sorrow. Visualise the Mahabharata in which divine charioteer Sri Krishna, ready to listen his friend Arjuna's directions. Seeing the great distinguished people like Bhishma and Daronacharya towards enemy side of Kauravas; Arjuna starts weakening with cowardly thoughts full of compassion with his mind depressed and eyes full of tears instead of getting prepared to fight the battle. Sri Krishna encouraged and inspired him for devotion of his duty to fight the battle and act as stepping stones for success.

The people are your important resource and if the people you work with, can become your loyal friends, they would be with you even in hell helping you to taste the success.

SECRETS OF BUSINESS SUCCESS

How can a business survive in a desperate competitive situation? Of course, it is possible by maintaining and improving the quality of product and services. We need to maintain spirit of service, fairness, harmony, cooperation, progress, courtesy, modesty and gratitude.

Business wisdom contain following secrets of success which is like making a gems necklace and hanging a pendant of ideas and thoughts:

(i) Successful companies are in business not solely for **money** but money is a by-product to them for doing the right things.

(ii) They manage for **consistent value creation, growth and profitability.** They have values since they know what they stand for and what is important. This reflects in the expectations of their employees.

(iii) They have **high value based cultures** which encourage people **to commit to the organisation and its goals.** This does not mean that the cultures are all enlightened and people-friendly. Sometimes they have cultures which are, in some ways, unpleasant.

(iv) They understand their **customers** needs, aspirations and behaviour. They develop strategies within a global context, consider global market opportunities and global competition threats.

(v) They are persistent and powerful communicators to ensure that the message gets through. People keep information and bring ideas to themselves or communicate with a select few. In the best companies, information and ideas are shared naturally and continually, which will encourage decisions faster, more innovative, matured, stronger and of greater value. They does not allow corporate politics to kill **communication.**

(vi) The great companies, great leaders and great entrepreneurs delight in **simplicity**. They cut needless waste and hierarchy but keep faith in simple practices and principles.

(vii) They are restlessly **creative to invent.** They go back to the beginning for a perennial state of reinvention. They push strategic thinking towards creation of new, innovative and breakthrough approaches.

(viii) They keep the people in **confidence** by constantly writing personal notes from top to bottom and keep the culture as well as values of the company on track.

(ix) They **earn lot of money** which is the happy result of above. Net profit is a by-product of excellence, not an end in itself.

(x) They develop **winning corporate strategies** and respond with speed and flexibility.

They realise that there is no other alternative except "keep on going; keep on going." Remembering that "life affords no higher pleasure than that of surmounting difficulties." We should not be disappointed by any set-back as "life is like a Rainbow: It needs both rain and sunshine to create the Colours."

SUCCESS OF THE ORGANISATION

Organisation exist for only one purpose: to help people reach ends together that they could not achieve individually. We all want an organisation that our people are proud of and committed to, where all employees have an opportunity to contribute, learn and grow on merit. We want our people to feel respected, treated fairly, listen to, and involved.

What makes an organisation sustainable and outstanding for success? **The passion for success and supremacy is key to sustainable competitive edge.** As you are aware, **the GLOBALISATION is the ability to compete in the world's market with an objective of generating more wealth for Organisation and Nation, to make it more prosperous. Every operation should be productive at all times.** Thus, today's success of the organisation will depend upon followings:

Particulars	*Style*
• Organisation	Market driven.
• People	Talented, confident, motivated, multi-skilled.
• Communication	Open.
• System	Simple, easy to use.
• Structure	Process / customer based.
• Technology	Cost effective, eco-friendly.
• Product	Innovative.

• Quality	Best.
• Culture	High value creation.
• Price	Right, competitive.
• Delivery	Prompt.
• Service	Efficient, customer friendly.

In order to be competitive and cost effective, you need to be MISER as follows:

M Merge operation.
I Improve activities.
S Simplify jobs.
E Eliminate repetition of jobs.
R Reduce operations.

"It is an immutable law in business that words are words, explanations are explanation, promises are promises—but only performance is reality." —*Harold Geneen*, Former CEO, ITT.

The performance management is the process for managing strategy of the organisation. It is how you translate plans into results. The key to improve is integrating and balancing multiple improvement methodologies.

The most important is passion for success and commitment to believe in values like honesty, integrity, customers value and innovation to translate strategy into results and action. There can be no compromise on values and organisation must be able to realise the talent and potential locked in their people and use this tremendous energy and enthusiasm for all-round success.

SUCCESS OF THE INDIVIDUAL

Performance of a person depends on his overall well being for which he should be physically fit, mentally alert and spiritually enlightened. In order to be successful in all areas of your life, you need to think healthy, wealthy, happy and successful through 24 hours a day and cancel all negative, destructive, fearful and unhappy thoughts. You invest your time in what you believe can succeed.

The following will create opportunities for success of the individuals:

(i) Develop and create a personal vision and be always eager to meet new challenges. Always keep the vision alive.

(ii) Develop ability to predict the future and to create it.

(iii) Guide creation of shared vision and getting everyone on the same wavelength.

(iv) Clearly define the objective to achieve the goals.

(v) Be focussed to go for growth in profit and volume.

(vi) Trust and faith to inspire, motivate and create enthusiasm in the entire work-force and drive people towards higher levels of efforts.

(vii) Ethical values to be trusted and never compromise on values. The best approach to future is to invent it on strength of ideas and creativity for value creation. **The continuous innovation is key to success.** Constantly encourage to innovate, experiment and breakthrough approach.

(viii) Create intellectual capital—manage talent and high potential individuals. Get best people around you and let them function.

(ix) New ideas—come with me—people come first and finally try this. Restructure the core team, if needed. Mobilise individuals towards a vision and build emotional bonds for the future.

(x) Do the tough things which no one else want to do.

(xi) Create cost optimisation and continuous cost reduction but maintain quality level of world standards.

(xii) Listen to your customers, employees, dealers and suppliers and create open communication system.

(xiii) Devote energy to consider when to listen and when to speak, when to act and when to observe.

(xiv) Create new customers.

(xv) Improve customer service. A satisfied customer is the best advertisement for the products.

(xvi) Enhance competitiveness and upgrade competencies.

(xvii) Ensure operational excellence in all areas to improve over-all performance.

(xviii) Create intelligent, resourceful and innovative management techniques as the hallmarks for success.

(xix) Invest in education to achieve global leadership. Continue to enhance the return on human capital.

(xx) Organise to operate in situation of continuous uncertainty.

(xxi) Achieve highest productivity, highest efficiency with consistency in quality upgradation at the right price, on time, each time for its customers.

The individual must have a passion and commitment to make their company one of the best managed and the largest in the world. They must have a burning desire to achieve ambitious goals and convert the constraints into opportunities to grow their business and add value. The clear vision, mission, goals and purpose should be in the hearts and minds of the individuals to develop competencies and competitiveness. Success is all around you, needing only an open mind and keen eye. Success demands a price. The greater the success, the higher the price. It is always better to pay the price of success than to suffer the cost of failure. In the end, it would be fair to say that the sincerity cannot be claimed, trust cannot be enforced, respect cannot be conditional, achievements cannot be counterfeit, purpose cannot be confused and success cannot be avoided.

Index